June Jones

NW

and

THEN

NOW AND THEN

June Jones

ISBN (Print Edition): 978-1-66781-594-7

ISBN (eBook Edition): 978-1-66781-595-4

"Yesterday is history, tomorrow is a mystery, and today is a gift; that's why they call it the present"

Eleanor Roosevelt

1

I find it virtually impossible to acknowledge that I am growing old, much less that I actually am old. While the calendar confirms I am no longer young, that I have reached the final phase of my life on earth, my mind and heart consistently reject the perception of myself as a truly senior citizen. Because I have enjoyed, and continue to enjoy, an exceptionally fortunate life, I tend to minimize the unknowable future, choosing instead to concentrate upon and be grateful for my present and my past. As I age, my mind increasingly blends yesterday's memories and today's events with a restrained preview of tomorrow's prospects.

I have always been introspective, but when I began to chronicle my life, to reexamine my past, I realized my choices were frequently motivated by emotions of which I was unaware, or failed to appreciate.

I have always been driven by an underlying desire and search for peace, for tranquility, coziness and physical comfort, by a longing for an absence of discomfort and the disagreeable. I have consistently sought the intimate rather than the grand, the simple rather than the complex, the enduring rather than the temporary, the reliable rather than the risk. Motivated by what I wished to avoid rather than by what I wished to attain, I have sought safety and security and pursued an absence of negatives rather than the acquisition of positives. My craving for warmth and affection manifested in a desire for all things cozy. Even if I could afford to reside in a grand mansion, I prefer a snug residence. For me, comfort is preferable to grandeur; cheerful colors are more appealing than somber hues.

While neither my father nor my Uncle Harry—the men who supervised and safeguarded my family and me—were exceptionally tall, in my search for security in a potential mate I invariably gravitated toward lanky long-limbed suitors. My favorite escorts were all well over six feet tall; one was six-foot-seven. An emotionally vulnerable, fragile five-foot-four, I always felt most comfortable, most sheltered and secure, in the company of towering, physically imposing men.

Although I loved my mother, I did not wish to be like her. A number of the traits she and I shared were characteristics I did not appreciate in myself. I regretted inheriting some of her shortcomings. Although mother was a determined Pisces and I am a flexible Gemini, all too often, her frailties—especially her stubbornness and shyness—became my liabilities.

I am typically Gemini; there are conflicting versions of June Jones. I have contradictory personalities: the fundamental at-home-alone-completely-natural-somewhat-vulnerable me, and the slightly artificial, seemingly self-assured, public me. Comfortable and casual in my residence, when preparing to go out, I am an actress readying for her roll on stage. Some days I wish to be noticed; some days, I prefer to be overlooked. I select my makeup, garments, and accessories accordingly. I may wish to appear prosperous or important, or prefer to seem humble or bland. I may attempt to look younger and more innocent, potentially more vulnerable, or older and more accomplished.

I am a city girl with a country heart. Raised and at ease amid continuous pressure, imbued with metropolitan necessitated skills and habits, I have always found compensatory relaxation in rural environments. As I age and hectic cities become more challenging, I favor a more countrified life. Having moved from the Northeast to Florida, instead of honking horns, I enjoy the murmur of songbirds; instead of skyscrapers, crowded streets, and grimy air, my windows embrace palm trees, bougainvillea, and a rushing stream.

2

I consider aging a cautious condition. Although I do not feel like an old lady, I have begun to behave like an old lady. No longer adventurous, I find comfort in the commonplace. Due to precaution, if not necessity, my environment and my habits are adjusting. Physical surroundings are becoming more secure; physical activities are becoming more circumspect. Increasingly, as habits change, my values and my cautions change. To quote television's Dr. Ruth Westheimer, "do not retire, rewire." I prepare for the worst but pray for and anticipate the best.

As attention-attracting clothing becomes less suitable, my manner of dress is becoming more restrained, more age-appropriate. I have replaced my stiletto heels with less challenging footwear. Because maneuvering tiny buttons through buttonholes has become more difficult, I opt for zippers, snaps, and Velcro. As occasions that require formal attire become fewer and more casual, my evening gowns and elegant jewelry remain sequestered in closets and a safe.

I find it reassuring, even comforting, to reside in a retirement community where neighbors and caregivers are familiar with varying degrees of decline. I am aware that my self-evaluation may differ from more objective observations. Reluctantly, while making charitable allowances for increasing shortcomings in my acquaintances, I am obliged to make comparable allowances for myself.

I read somewhere that while one's body knows how old one is, one's mind refuses to believe it. How true! To quote one of my neighbors, her "get-up-and-go has got up and went." Another asserts that she has reached the snapdragon stage; part of her has snapped, the rest of her is draggin'." A friend's tee-shirt declares that "It's weird being the same age as old people." and an acquaintance comments that "old is when your body dries up or leaks."

One acquaintance recommends we forgo health foods, reasoning that we have reached the stage in life where we need all of the preservatives we can get. Another comments that "It's hard to be nostalgic when you can't remember anything." Yet another quotes a perceptive poem proclaiming:

I get used to my arthritis,

to my dentures I'm resigned,

I can manage my bifocals,

but God I miss my mind!

It is primarily my memory—the unreliability of my memory—that exasperates me. All too often, having entered a room purposefully, I cannot remember what the purpose was. To keep keys, eyeglasses, jewelry, and the like from being lost, I stow them away carefully, then cannot recall where I have placed them. Upon encountering an old acquaintance, after we part I wonder who the hell was that? Fortuitously, thanks to mutual forgetfulness, it is becoming safe for me to share secrets with my companions; like me, they too will not remember.

When working at my computer, I do not feel elderly, I feel as though I am in my prime. Only when I move about, do I realize I am actually an old lady with increasingly limited abilities.

I used to entertain frequently; now, I wish to be entertained. I used to enjoy inviting people to attend assorted events; now, I enjoy being invited. I used to like creating and consuming elaborate meals; now, I prefer simpler, lighter fare prepared by someone other than myself.

Accepting and adjusting to life's changes can be intimidating. One customarily broadminded neighbor inadvertently attended a bawdy film in our local theatre. Offended by the crude scenes and raunchy dialogue, she wanted to leave but remained seated because she did not wish fellow movie-goers to consider her a bigot or a prude. Eventually, unable to abide the continuous vulgarity, she rose from her front-row seat and, turning toward the exit, realized she was alone in the theater. All of the other viewers had already escaped.

A sense of humor is essential. One friend insists that she will "never be over the hill" because she is far too weary to climb that hill. When asked by an acquaintance for her age, another friend replied, "I will be one-hundred in eight years."

Shortly before her death, a rapidly failing ninety-nine-year-old cheerfully advised the Hospice nurse, who was bathing her and arranging her hair, "A little powder, a little paint can make you look like what you ain't."

It is said that "age is a question of mind over matter; if one doesn't mind, it doesn't matter." One should not worry about getting old, only about thinking old.

Bernard Baruch once told my father that as he aged, "old" was becoming increasingly older. He considered "old" to be at least fifteen years beyond his current age. "Don't let aging get you down," he warned, "it's too hard to get up."

Actress Anne Bancroft opined that the best way to get most husbands to do something was to suggest that perhaps they were too old to do it.

When disclosing her years, my former neighbor, Jolie Gabor de Szigethy (glamorous mother of the high-profile Gabor sisters), invariably added a decade to her actual age. Asked why, she confessed that she wanted people to notice and admire her, to be impressed by how remarkable she seemed. Espousing a contrary point of view, comedian Lucile Ball agreed that "the secret to remaining young was to lie about one's age"—reducing it. Screen star Doris Day claimed that "the most frightening thing about middle age was the knowledge that inevitably one will grow out of it."

I do not reinvent my age. I have no desire to appear other than I am. Quite the contrary, I perceive advantages to evident maturation, to a hopefully youthful deportment accompanied by an increasingly elderly appearance. I welcome the consideration and concern, the added respect that advanced age engenders. While strangers continue to invite me to join in challenging enterprises, they also hold doors open to make way for me, offer me their seats in crowded venues, defer to my presumed needs and assumed acumen. Primarily an observer rather than a participant, a chronicler rather than an executer, I find a certain comfort in aging. Everyday challenges diminish because I am learning how to deal with them and, whenever possible, how to avoid them.

3

I am surprised by how much I have always taken for granted, by the extraordinary things I perceived as ordinary. My family's Park Avenue penthouse, my grandmother's chauffeured limousine, our fulsome meals, my mother's jewels, our deluxe vacations all seemed routine. Oblivious to the Depression, and the reality of my privileged life, my environment seemed unexceptional. Day-to-day surroundings and activities seemed commonplace. In my household, the variety of people I routinely encountered were simply people, familiar figures. Some of them may have seemed extraordinary to outsiders, but to me, they were merely family friends and acquaintances, their celebrity inconsequential.

When Queen Victoria's grandson, the Duke of Württemberg, visited, he was simply a pleasant gentleman, a close friend, and colleague of my father. What impressed me was the elegant royal seal that invariably embellished his letters. When noble prizewinner and architect of the nuclear age, Enrico Fermi, taught my third-grade class how to sing *Funiculi funicula* in Italian, and explained the Theory of Relativity, he was merely my classmate Nella's father. Another class parent, Abraham Epstein, was reputed to be the father and principal designer of the New Deal and Social Security. Another father owned Lionel Trains and my friend Anne Bernays' father (a nephew of Sigmund Freud) was considered the father of Public Relations. Mary Rodgers' father, Richard, was a successful composer. My own father, a businessman, did not impress me as being particularly noteworthy. I was unaware he was involved in the creation and deployment of the Atomic Bomb, or that he worked intermittently with both Secretary of State George Marshall and President Harry Truman, that he was instrumental in the development of chemically accurate synthetic sapphires, rubies, and emeralds.

As a smug three-year-old, when world-famous pianist Myra Hess played Mozart on our grand piano, I presumed to advise her that, although she played very well, the perforated rolls that one could insert into the piano required less effort and sounded better. Opinionated, even when too young to recognize and appreciate true talent, I regarded people and environments as familiar or unfamiliar, pleasant or unpleasant, entertaining or boring, approachable or avoidable.

I may balance my perceived inadequacies with other people's compensatory characteristics. To counter shortcomings, I may gravitate toward the bold versus the inhibited, the scientific versus the artistic, the accomplished versus the amateur, the extrovert versus the introvert, the demonstrative versus the constrained. For me, opposites are not necessarily incompatible; I recognize that disparities can be advantageous.

4

1931, the year of my birth, spawned a variety of significant events. Comic strip detective Dick Tracy, Disney's Donald Duck, and Rudolph the Red-Nosed Reindeer were also born that year. In March, the *Star-Spangled Banner* was adopted as our national anthem. In May, the Empire State Building (until 1970, the tallest building in the world) received its first occupants. The George Washington Bridge opened in October, and, overlooking Rio de Janeiro, the statue of Christ the Redeemer was christened. In New York City, the legendary Waldorf-Astoria Hotel moved to its ultimate location.

When it opened on Park Avenue, the Waldorf-Astoria was the largest, tallest, and most expensive hotel in the world. Considered to be one of the most exclusive, it was responsible for numerous innovations. Room service originated at the Waldorf. The hotel's famous chef, Oscar, invented such popular culinary creations as Waldorf Salad, Eggs Benedict, Thousand Island Dressing, Veal Oscar, and Red Velvet Cake. Rob Roy and Bobbie Burns cocktails were created in the hotel's Sir Harry's Bar. As a teenager beginning to mature socially, it was at the Waldorf that I gained confidence while dancing with shy, pimply-faced boys; where I learned to feel at ease in elegant ball gowns enhanced by requisite orchid or gardenia corsages. Together with Radio City Music Hall and the 1939-40 New York World's

Fair—all of which glamorized Art Deco—the Waldorf was at least partially responsible for my lifelong affection for that discipline.

When I learned the hotel was destined for renovation into a costly condominium-com-guesthouse, I felt a profound sense of loss, of having aged, of having outlived yet another presumed permanent, but now potentially perishable, landmark. Memories ensued: recollections of lavish charity balls; of Starlight Roof New Year's Eve celebrations, with music by Guy Lombardo and his Royal Canadians, of being entertained in the hotel's Empire Room and Peacock Alley by Maurice Chevalier, Edith Piaf, and a variety of other notable performers.

The year of my birth also introduced numerous products destined to become commonplace. Electric shavers. aerosol cans and nylon fabric made their debut. Alka Seltzer began providing relief to thousands. AT&T debuted its ubiquitous Teletype machines.

Across the world, Spain converted from a monarchy to a republic. The city of New Delhi replaced Calcutta as the capital of British-India. Australia, New Zealand, Canada, Newfound, Ireland, and South Africa became independent members of the British Commonwealth.

During 1931, the world remained in the throws of the Great Depression. The Dow Jones Industrial Average fell from 169 to a fraction over 77. Although my father's companies teetered on bankruptcy, thanks to the sagacity and guidance of mother's financially astute brother Harry, her more than adequate inherited assets remained intact, and neither my parents nor I ever suffered significant hardship.

5

I have known a surprising number of people with whom I shared a June ninth birthday. Curiously, two who became close friends were midlife next-door neighbors residing in apartments immediately adjacent to mine. The first, in Palm Beach, Florida, was Lois Field; the second, after I moved to Palm Beach Gardens, was Don Lewis. In each instance, we had traits and interests in common. Sharing a profound fondness for foreign travel, we were all passionate art collectors who amassed fine, often exotic, *objects de virtue.*

Another friend, Charlotte Jablin, whom I initially met aboard a cruise ship, lived nearby. With a mutual enthusiasm for worldwide travel and husbands who also became friends, we shared more than a birthdate. Having acquired an extensive collection of eyeglasses that encompassed an infinite variety of shapes and colors, both of us were known by our spectacles. Our glasses always complemented our clothing and were so numerous they necessitated their own small suitcases when we traveled. Eyeglasses were our mutual, self-promoting means of identity.

Still another enduring travel-initiated friendship involved an erudite couple who assiduously "collected countries" in an attempt to visit every nation on earth. The husband, also born on the ninth of June, introduced me to the Travelers Century Club, members of which have visited at least one hundred countries. Having spent time in more than one-hundred-and-forty nations, I have long since been eligible to join the group, but, as yet, have not done so.

I have also shared my birthday with three maternal relatives. One, whom I met only once, was an elderly German lady who, having survived the Holocaust, lived with her descendants in northern California. My additional birthdate sharing cousins, both of whom were a generation older than me, were my friends. Elsie, who survived for a healthy one hundred and two years, was fiercely independent. An internationally renowned bridge champion and teacher, she taught me to play the game, enabling me to enjoy many years of capable competition. She also fostered my friendship with her niece, Gertrude Schmeidler, a cousin with whom I shared a protracted, occasionally professional involvement in the occult.

Despite enjoying very different lifestyles, my other birthday-sharing cousin, George Goman, and I had similar talents and enthusiasms. George was a competitive world-class tennis player, while I, a shy and reluctant teenager, demurred when encouraged to practice and compete in the US Open championships at Forest Hills. George and I were both gadget buffs, frequently ferreting out and acquiring promising, state-of-the-art devices. Thanks to George, I viewed my first domestic television set with its minuscule fuzzy black and white images. He and I were both avid art collectors, sharing a love of beauty and amassing an assortment of treasures. We both loved to write and did so professionally. George penned a popular gossip column and restaurant reviews for a distinguished Los Angeles newspaper. I wrote and edited articles for various national publications, including Harpers Bazaar, and a technical aeronautical periodical where aviator Charles Lindberg was my boss. In the 1960s, under the auspices of then-President Juscelino Kubitschek, I wrote a book about Brazil, which was translated into Portuguese by Jorge Amado, the acclaimed Brazilian novelist. Leery of potential negative political ramifications, I withdrew the manuscript from its publisher, Editora Globo, and it was never printed. My memoir, *Chance Encounters*, published several years ago, has sold modestly in bookstores in both the United States and Brazil.

In the 1960s, during one of my more leisurely strolls along Manhattan's Madison Avenue, I happened to pause outside an interesting antique shop. Bright sunlight reflected off its large window, displaying a clear image of me standing alongside another woman in similar dress. In the mirrored reflection, she and I looked so remarkably alike that, turning to one another, we laughed and introduced ourselves, commenting that we resembled twins. The charming, extremely friendly lady was Happy Rockefeller. Although she was the recent second wife of then-Governor Nelson Rockefeller, with whom I was well acquainted, she and I had never met. Subsequently, I learned that, although Happy was a few years my senior, she and I not only looked and dressed alike, we shared a birthday.

There appears to be validity to the dictums of the zodiac, the premise that those who share a sign share common characteristics. We June 9th Geminis had both physical and dispositional traits in common. Years ago, identified simply as "Miss Hirsch," I was introduced to movie star, Rock Hudson. After only a few minutes, Rock asked whether I had been born on June 7th, 8th, or 9th. Startled, I asked him why he had inquired and Rock replied that because he found me so typically Gemini, he assumed I must have been born on or near the middle of the sign.

6

Innate Gemini ambivalence, accompanied by youthful exposure to life's diversity and contradictions, may account for the degree to which I appreciate conflicting, even controversial, aspects of an issue. Differing personalities and emotions have always intrigued me. I do not isolate myself, nor permit myself to be become bored by banality. My world is enlarged and enhanced by variety, by the unknown, the unfamiliar, by the unanticipated. I am cautious but unafraid, curious but careful.

As a preschooler, my live-in nanny was an undemonstrative, anorexic, ash-blond German who, although efficient, was remote and unemotional. She intimidated me. Although she taught me how to dress and feed myself, how to read, enjoy drawing, playing with blocks, and solitaire, she made me feel insecure and inadequate. I believed she was a Nazi sympathizer. Alternatively, when my family visited certain friends, the couple's obese black housekeeper looked after me with unrestrained affection. She was warm, animated, and upbeat. I adored her. She made me feel important and loved. The contrast with *fräulein* was edifying. While both caretakers nurtured me, the occasional caregiver's warmth and coddling, her intimacy, made me yearn for a full-time, lovable Negro nanny.

When I was only five, my father, with his lifelong commercial and emotional attachments to Brazil, inculcated me with a profound affection for and identification with that country. Although it is a large nation, I have always thought of Brazil as a small world, a welcoming world of privileged families and friends.

Having spent considerable time in South America, periodically residing in the homes of two prominent Brazilian families, I consider myself at least partially Brazilian. As a guest of the de Sá family in Salvador da Bahia and the Ribeiro family in São Paulo, I always felt like a genuine member of each household. Because my hosts significantly influenced my emotions, personality, and behavior, I consider myself to be the extremely fortunate member of three families, two Brazilian, one North American. My biological family's Manhattan penthouse, the de Sá's fruit tree shaded home, and the Ribeiro's suburban villa always seemed equally cozy and familiar, equally warm and hospitable: equally where I belonged.

I grew up both impressed and influenced by the contrast between what I viewed as South American tradition and North American innovation, between the seemingly old-fashioned and the more venturesome. Brazilian customs and attitudes, divergent from those of North America, had a considerable effect on me.

In my youth, the de Sá residence in Bahia had two functioning kitchens. One was a large, state-of-the-art, mid-century modern area equipped with contemporary appliances, including an electric mixer and a gas range. It was the space in which mother and daughters enjoyed concocting impressive modern dishes. The alternative kitchen, installed around a wood-burning stove, was where the servants, employing primitive tools (such as a crude stone pestle and mortar), prepared most of our meals. The sole contemporary concession in the more antiquated venue was an electric refrigerator, placed alongside a still functioning, if obsolete, icebox. Because the rice and beans, the *bifes,* and cocoanut infused desserts prepared in both kitchens were equally delicious, I realized that divergence could confirm the positive potential in nonconformity.

Whether influenced by North or South America, by Jewish or Catholic traditions, my food cravings became diversified. My perception of home cooking and comfort foods became bi-national. To this day, I find *feijoada* (Brazilian black bean stew), *goiabada con queijo* (guava jelly with cheese), mangos, and cocoanut as routine, as appealing and emotionally satisfying as chicken soup with matzo balls, lox, chopped chicken liver, and kosher hot dogs.

7

Not only did I inherit my love of Brazilian food, Brazil, and Brazilians from my father, upon his death, I inherited his sprawling *fazenda* (ranch), a remote northern property slightly larger in area than Manhattan Island.

I never visited the territory. Only sixteen when my father passed away, I was considered a foolish female, naïve, and uninformed. Without consulting me, Daddy's executors disposed of the acreage at a regrettably undervalued price. The well-intentioned men were unaware that, young as I was, I was not merely an unwary, ineffectual female; I was in serious communication with a potential buyer, an internationally prominent European billionaire who had sought me out, interested in acquiring and renovating territory in the under-developed heartland of Brazil.

While my income from various inherited Brazilian investments continued to accrue, due to both practical and financial concerns, exporting that income to the United States was deemed inadvisable. To hedge devaluation, I invested the accumulating currency in IBEC, the International Basic Economy Corporation of the Rockefeller Foundation, and became a friend of the fund's administrator, Nelson Rockefeller. Taking me under his wing, Nelson lured me into politics, moderately liberal New York Republican politics. Nelson also took pleasure in introducing me to eligible bachelors, enhancing and advancing my post-college social life.

At a Rockefeller cocktail reception during a campaign to promote the election of John Vliet Lindsay to Congress, I was introduced to a debonair fellow volunteer. The young man and I chatted amiably, and when the twilight gathering concluded, he offered to escort me home. He seemed charming and harmless enough so, upon reaching my residence, I invited him to my apartment for a nightcap.

Once upstairs, the fellow no longer seemed quite so harmless. As we removed our coats he began to chase me around the apartment, seeking far more intimate attention than I was willing to provide. I was having difficulty fending him off when he stopped abruptly in front of an étagère that held, among other antiquities, a baroque Brazilian statue of the Madonna and a timeworn Greek icon depicting the mother of Christ.

"I thought you were Jewish?" he demanded questioningly.

"I am."

"Then what the hell are you doing with two images of the Virgin?" Obviously, he disapproved.

Thinking quickly, I replied, "Why for me, they're like the boot hanging over the shoemaker's door and the pretzel above the entrance to a pastry shop --- they identify my house."

Visibly deflated, he groaned, grabbed his overcoat, mumbled "Sorry," and fled.

Ave Maria!

8

I used to enjoy strolling along Madison Avenue. On its sidewalks and within its various eateries and boutiques, I routinely spotted familiar, often notable figures. Some were inconspicuous, while others made eye contact, even smiled or mumbled a passing greeting. Lunching in a neighborhood coffee shop, I occasionally shared a nod and a banquette, if not a table, with acclaimed scientist Carl Sagan. During manicures at a Madison Avenue beauty parlor, I would sit alongside songstress Eartha Kitt and exchange greetings with newsman David Brinkley when he came to call for his freshly coifed wife. As a fellow art and auction addict, I became the casual acquaintance of accused, convicted, but ultimately exonerated, murder suspect Claus von Bülow. Other neighborhood sightings included a lean, inconspicuously garbed figure exhibiting what I took to be decisively masculine body language. Eventually, I realized that the trouser-clad figure I had presumed to be an athletic young man was, in reality, a partially disguised middle-aged woman, the enigmatic, deliberately inconspicuous, remarkably handsome Greta Garbo.

Literally, as well as figuratively, Madison Avenue played a propitious roll in my life. Not merely as a convenient thoroughfare where I regularly ran into old friends and casual acquaintances, but as a metaphor for the availability and commerce of fine art. The avenue was where I encountered, learned to appreciate, and occasionally purchased a variety of collectibles. There, exposed to fellow art devotees with mutual interests and enthusiasms, was where I established numerous friendships and was captivated by and into the world of art and artists.

Waiting to complete a purchase following a sale at Sotheby-Parke-Burnet, when the auction house was still located on Madison Avenue, I met the woman who became my closest friend. Chatting casually, I collected my Picasso etching; and Susan, an oriental antique dealer, acquired an imperial cinnabar box that came into my possession some sixteen years later, following Susan's untimely death from cancer.

I was also befriended by the rather stuffy widowed owner of a prestigious Madison Avenue art gallery. He courted me, wanting to marry me I surmised, not for my looks or personality, but for what, because I was an avid, if modest, art collector, he incorrectly assumed was my considerable wealth.

One of my earliest art instigated friends was Harold Hart, principal salesman and eventual director of the prestigious Martha Jackson gallery. Charming, knowledgeable, and patient, Harold taught me about the ins and outs of contemporary painting, and introduced me intellectually, then socially, to such emerging color field and abstract expressionist artists as Paul Jenkins, Robert Natkin, Sam Francis, Jules Olitski, and Louise Nevelson. Among the Nevelson pieces I own is one Louise gave me as a thank you gift, in appreciation of my donation to a charity of mutual interest. The authenticity of another of my Nevelson's (a multiple) has been questioned because it boasts a signature, even though that series was never signed. Present when I purchased it, Louise had graciously inscribed the piece for me.

Provenances can be surprising, elusive, even disquieting. One of my prized possessions is a tall, slender earthenware urn annotated in black ink and autographed by Moshe Dayan, who had exhumed it. Years after acquiring the vessel from a reputable Madison Avenue gallery, I learned of the relic's previously disguised but factual history. My fourth-century Roman remnant, erstwhile possession of the Israeli government, had been stolen, smuggled out of Israel, and sold surreptitiously, possibly by the very gentleman who had unearthed and signed it.

9

Inadvertently, in addition to my innocent purchase and possession of stolen property, I ran afoul of the law on at least one other occasion. I stole an automobile.

During the early 1950s, in the tranquil and trusting Adirondack resort communities where I spent my summers, everyone left their car keys inside their unattended, unlocked vehicles. While on vacation one sun-drenched afternoon, I parked my Ford near neighborhood courts and played tennis. Upon retrieving the vehicle, I drove into town some twenty miles distant to run a few errands. Upon returning to the car, chores completed, and shivering from a sudden chill in the air, I reached into the sedan's rear compartment to retrieve my pink, in-case-I-need-it sweater. The seat was empty! Fearing theft, it was only when I glanced at the license plate that I realized that *I* had been the thief. I had commandeered a car that looked like mine but belonged to someone else. Fearful, lest I be pursued and apprehended by the police, I drove to the local stationhouse, confessed my guilt, and advised the Sergeant that I would return the automobile to its original parking space forthwith. Scowling reproachfully for a moment, the officer began to laugh and sent me on my way.

In 1963, on July fourth, I had a dinner date with friends at a restaurant in a rather dubious part of Manhattan. Before leaving home, due to one of my vivid extra-sensory premonitions, I removed a favorite ring that I was wearing and hid it in a dresser draw amid piles of crumpled lingerie. The diamond-enhanced band was not only valuable, but a sentimental favorite because its huge pearl had served as my late father's favorite tiepin. Forewarned that the gem was about to be stolen, I removed it from my finger and secreted it. Satisfied the jewel was safe, I departed, joined friends, and enjoyed a leisurely evening downtown.

When I returned home, something seemed amiss. I had left the apartment in a rather cluttered state, with odds and ends of papers and apparel scattered about. My home looked immaculate; clothing had been neatly folded, papers stacked and thoughtfully put away. I rushed to my dresser. My drawers had been tidied, but my ring, along with additional jewelry, had vanished. My premonition had come true but not in the manner that I had envisioned. The burglar had not attacked me, but had ransacked my home and had been far neater than me in the attempted cover-up.

While the thief was eventually apprehended, none of my missing jewelry, including an extremely valuable diamond and platinum broach, was recovered. When I reported the theft to my insurance company, I received surprising instructions. Since I had a clear photograph and accurate measurements of the purloined pin, they directed me to have the piece duplicated by a jeweler of the insurers' choice. If, when ready, the replication did not please me, or, following evaluation by an independent appraiser, was determined to be worth less than the pilfered piece, I was to reject the replacement, and the insurance value of the original would be returned to me in cash.

Upon completion, the new broach was virtually indistinguishable from the original, but the stones were slightly larger and of even finer quality. The substitute, which I wear to this day, is worth considerably more than the pin that I had lost. Who says that "crime doesn't pay?"

10

I have been privileged to converse with a number of First Ladies. In addition to visiting Dona Sarah Kubitschek and her husband in their country home above Rio de Janeiro during Juscelino's tenure as President of Brazil, I have chatted with six First Ladies of the United States.

I met Eleanor Roosevelt on two widely separate occasions. She was a resident of the White House and a guest lecturer at my elementary school when I accidentally collided with her in a slippery corridor. As I tumbled to the ground, she graciously lifted me off the floor and comforted me. I encountered her again in my twenties, shortly after her retirement as a delegate to the United Nations. For a reason I can no longer recall, I was assigned to deliver a packet of confidential papers to her home office --- documents she had requested for her syndicated newspaper column *My Day*. To my surprise, when I rang the bell of the townhouse on East 65th Street, it was Mrs. Roosevelt herself who came to the service entrance (rather than the front door), inviting me into her kitchen, where we chatted pleasantly over a tumbler of milk and some chocolate chip cookies. Mrs. Roosevelt was warm and gracious. Shy as I was at the time, she was not at all intimidating.

Shortly after she became First Lady, I met Lady Bird Johnson in a gynecologist's stuffy waiting room. Seemingly anxious about her apparently impromptu visit, she distracted herself by regaling two fellow patients and me with an abundance of amusing anecdotes and asides. She was easy-going, animated, and compatible.

I ran into Patricia Nixon on several occasions before she moved into the White House. I first saw her in 1951, between acts of Aida on the opening night of the Metropolitan Opera season. At the time her husband (who was not with her that night) was the junior Senator from California. I had no idea whom she might be but was instantly attracted by her beauty. She was standing near me, chatting with designer Oleg Cassini and his date, actress Grace Kelly. Although Kelly looked as lovely as always, her beauty seemed overshadowed by the even lovelier (and far more becomingly dressed) Mrs. Nixon. Nine years later, while working with Vice President Nixon during his initial presidential campaign, I was privileged to spend time with Pat on a number of occasions. She seemed shy but appreciative of the opportunity to retreat into our casual engagements.

While shopping for clothing at Saks Fifth Avenue in Beverley Hills, I had a fleeting encounter with Nancy Reagan. Visiting California, I and had gone to Saks to shop for clothing. Wearing one of their newest outfits, I was browsing in the St. John boutique when a manager grabbed my arm, ushered me out of the boutique, and into a small, adjacent area that had been rearranged to host an elegant luncheon. Upon entry, I was gifted with a decorative bag of small but expensive items, greeted like the celebrity I wasn't, and escorted to the receiving line where I was presented to the event's guest of honor: First Lady Nancy Reagan (who, by coincidence, happened to be wearing a bright red version of the same royal blue suit that I was wearing). Perplexed, and somewhat disconcerted, I surmised that because I was dressed in one of host St John's newest outfits, enhanced by respectable jewelry, I was presumed to be a duly invited guest. Placed in a seat across the luncheon table from a gracious Mrs. Reagan, I felt uncomfortably self-conscious and slipped away as quickly as was feasible, puzzled by the dubious efficiency of the First Lady's security detail.

While attending a fashionable art and antique show in New York City, I was approached by then Vice-Presidential wife, Barbara Bush. We were both admiring the same exhibit when she engaged me in an enthusiastic conversation about various items in the display. As we chatted, a pad-and-pencil baring woman approached, asking Mrs. Bush for her autograph. Laughing, Mrs. Bush responded that she was "a nobody," it was her husband, former head of the CIA, and current Vice-President, who was famous, but even he was "not all that important." The future First Lady and eventual "First Mother" was lovely to look at, and I enjoyed our conversation. With apparent underlying strength and self-assurance, her friendly manner and her modesty all seemed genuine.

In 1996, board member of a local Palm Beach hospital, I attended the dedication of its newly enlarged cancer center whose supervising physician was a female and the mother of young children. Hillary Clinton was the keynote speaker at the ribbon-cutting ceremony. She spoke beautifully and without notes or hesitation. When the formalities concluded, as prearranged by a mutual acquaintance, I made my way toward the dais to meet the First Lady. As I approached, I overheard someone from her security detail urging her to leave for her next engagement. "No," she declared firmly, there were a number of people with whom she wished to talk. Even so, she would meet with no one until she had spoken with the medical director's children. The youngsters, over-awed by the important visitor, were cowering timidly nearby. The youngest, a girl about two years of age, influenced by her older siblings, was weeping, trembling, and attempting to hide. As I watched, Mrs. Clinton approached the anxious trio and reached out to them. Within seconds the little girl leapt into the First Lady's arms, laughing and kissing and clinging to her. Her brother and sister seemed to be equally entranced. "You can't fool a two-year-old," I thought to myself. Unlike her cool and disciplined public image, Mrs. Clinton appeared to be a genuinely warm and loving person. By chance, I had been privileged to peek beyond the woman's familiar facade and glimpse her soft and gentle side. When Hillary finally turned to greet me, we enjoyed a delightful, gossipy discussion about mutual friends, fashion choices, and local events. The conversation even included confidential whispered advice on where and how to shop for bargains. Noticing the designer suit I was wearing, she admired it. Adding that she hoped I had not paid full price for the outfit, she scribbled a note with the address and phone number of a source, where, citing her recommendation, I could purchase St. Johns at a significant discount.

The following year, I attended an intimate Palm Beach luncheon where Mrs. Clinton, still First Lady, was guest of honor. I was privileged to enjoy another leisurely conversation with her. Once again, she was extremely easy to chat with. She had a delightful, quick, playful, and, I suspected, potentially wicked sense of humor. Once again, in addition to her obvious intelligence and acute memory, she impressed me as being very warm, approachable, and down to earth. She seemed genuinely curious and empathetic, a genuine "people person," someone who listened, who remembered, who cared.

My most recent encounter with Hillary occured during her candidacy for President of the United States. Privileged to spend renewed time with the former First Lady/Secretary of State, I found her as astute, as likeable and as comfortable to associate with as ever.

11

In addition to six First Ladies, I have met and interacted—at least briefly—with eight heads of state: seven of them from the United States, the eighth from Brazil. I encountered three of the men—Eisenhower, Clinton, and Kubitschek—on numerous occasions before, during, and after each one's presidency. I met two of the men—Nixon and Johnson—while they were serving as vice-president, and the remaining three—Truman, Kennedy, and Carter—either before or after they held office.

During August of 1954, I narrowly missed spending an entire day with yet another head of state, President Getúlio Vargas of Brazil. A family friend had invited me to cruise the South Atlantic aboard his yacht, along with his chum and golfing buddy, Vargas. Tragically, the encounter was not to be. On the day before our scheduled voyage, Vargas was found dead, shot through the heart, purportedly by his own hand. Despite retrieval of an eloquent suicide note, my intended host, along with several other insiders, believed a carefully disguised assassination was the actual cause of the controversial President's demise.

I cannot remember how I first encountered Kubitschek, but during Juscelino's presidency, he wrote both the foreword and the cover-commentary for a book I was writing about Brazil. While still in office, he and his wife Dona Sara entertained me in their summer residence and, during a visit to the United States, dined with me in my New York apartment, where I courageously prepared the elegant formal dinner myself.

All the heads of state I have been privileged to encounter impressed me with their distinctive personalities. Each emitted an aura of self-confidence and self-assurance. With the exception of Eisenhower (due to his commanding war record), and Lyndon Banes Johnson (because I found him arrogant and offensive), all of the leaders seemed like ordinary human beings. Encounters were casual and comfortable rather than high profile and powerful.

On several occasions after leaving office, former President Truman approached me in the street, or the lobby of his New York City hotel, The Carlyle. Ever curious, he wished to learn about my personal feelings and my generation's opinions on current and controversial world affairs. Always gracious, when initiating our original encounter, he introduced himself by reassuring me that he was "a gentleman, not a masher."

I met then General Eisenhower for the first time during a luncheon following the triumphant parade that welcomed him home upon his return from the Second World War. Years later, during one of my numerous encounters with him as President, I inadvertently witnessed him engaged in a somewhat rancorous argument with a reluctantly respectful Vice-President Nixon.

In 1960, as an official member of Nixon's advance team during his presidential campaign opposite Kennedy, I chatted with the candidate and his delightful, if timid, wife, and daughters on several occasions.

During the 1950s, I frequented the home of Cordelia Mellon Scaife, whose property was situated at the north end of Palm Beach, immediately south of Ambassador Joseph Kennedy's Florida retreat. Cordy and I enjoyed sunbathing and relaxing on the sand that abutted her home and the adjacent

Kennedy estate. The beach was where she and I used to encounter three of her next-door neighbors, the friendly, if rambunctious, Kennedy brothers. At one time or another, John and Bobby each invited me out for an evening of dining and dancing. Young and innocent as I was, I was only modestly flattered by their attention. I knew better than to accept. My friends and I were well aware that, even on a first date, going out with a Kennedy would be tantamount to risking and, willingly or not, losing one's virginity.

Although I felt that Lyndon Johnson was a good president, I detested him and considered him a dreadful human being. Due to a series of unfortunate circumstances in an extremely crowded venue in Athens, Greece, then Vice-President Johnson, stepping backward, landed on one of my feet, fracturing a bone in my instep. Inadvertently, I cried out in pain! I did not recognize the offending gentleman from behind. But when Johnson neither acknowledged nor apologized for injuring me, I retaliated by kicking him vigorously in his shin with the sharp metal heel of my shoe, only to be constrained as a potential assassin by surrounding Secret Service officers. Fortunately, because of my previous associations with Eisenhower and Nixon, I held a top security clearance. When a nearby agent, recognizing me, vouched for my innocence, I was released from custody. Only recently, I learned that Jackie Kennedy shared my long-held suspicion that it was LBJ who actually arranged the murder of JFK.

Jimmy Carter and I met at a cocktail party in Manhattan during his campaign for the presidency. He impressed me as being likable, intelligent, and kind. When it was requested that he be my overnight houseguest during intermittent New York City portions of his quest for office, I hesitated; not relishing the inconvenience I declined.

Bill Clinton, whom I have met frequently under a variety of circumstances, has always projected immense charm. Charisma is an interesting phenomenon. Although I have found both Clintons extremely charismatic, I find them charismatic in entirely different ways.

Projecting warmth, ease, and genuine interest, Hillary's demeanor has always suggested familiarity, giving the illusion of intimacy and longstanding friendship. She made me feel we were old friends who shared a casual, yet lengthy history with compatible thoughts and feelings. Even in a crowded room, Bill always made me feel that he and I were alone, the only people in a jam-packed venue; that he liked me, was genuinely interested in me and my opinions; that he wanted to get to know me better, to learn more about me and my outlook on life. While both Clintons made me feel that I was important, and important to them, one seemed to have been part of my past, to have always known me, to have shared an extended friendship; the other ostensibly wanted to get to know me better, to become part of my future as my devoted and caring friend. One-on-one, each exuded a distinctive magnetism, a powerful yet entirely different pseudo intimacy.

12

Because I was never a good chauffeur, and intensely disliked driving, taxies provided a recurrent mode of transportation for me in whatever city I happened to find myself. Taxies and taxi drivers frequently added both interest and amusement to my life.

About to return to the United States from São Paulo at the end of a particularly lengthy sojourn in Brazil, I telephoned for a car to take me to the airport. During the preceding months, I had employed an assortment of local drivers to transport me about the city. To my amazement, when my requested airdrome transportation arrived, my car was accompanied by a group of additional, passenger-free, taxies. A few of my customary chauffeurs had decided to give me, their frequent North American patron, a grand, horn-honking escort to the airfield, and a festive, balloon enhanced farewell.

One stormy evening, in the lobby of my family's Manhattan residence, I ran into author Tennessee Williams, who had been dining in a neighbor's apartment. We were both waiting in the building's downstairs lobby, hoping the doorman, despite a torrential downpour, would find each of us a taxi. Chatting as we waited, we realized we were both heading to the 92nd Street Y to hear mellifluous-voiced Dylan Thomas recite his poetry. Eventually, and with much difficulty, the doorman managed to procure a taxi, and we rode off together. Williams was friendly, talkative, and surprisingly comfortable to chat with. We sat together at the recital and when it concluded, Tennessee introduced me to Thomas.

Visiting Las Vegas in the 1950s, I hailed a cab in front of my hotel and was descending onto the car's rear seat when comedian Jack Benny approached and asked whether, due to a dearth of taxies, he might share my ride. Surprised, but feeling perfectly safe, I agreed, and Benny sank onto the front seat beside the driver. To my surprise, in light of the comedian's parsimonious reputation, Mr. Benny insisted upon paying for both his trip and mine, handing the driver a very generous tip.

Back in New York, having exited the Bonwit Teller department store at the height of the afternoon rush hour, I was fortunate to commandeer a taxi and jumped inside via the left-hand passenger door. At precisely the same moment, former President Nixon's daughter Tricia Nixon Cox, believing she was the one who had successfully hailed the cab, entered through the right-hand door. She laughed and, recognizing me from the distant past, suggested that, since cabs were scarce and the day unpleasantly hot, we share the ride. We did. The trip was most enjoyable. As always, she was compatible and charming.

My most unlikely cab driver was not really a cab driver at all. Nor, from the erratic, inept way he drove, should he have been. Visiting my mother in Florida in the early 1950s, I descended to the taxi/limousine section of her hotel's parking lot seeking a ride into town. It was lunchtime and a group of idle drivers in their shirtsleeves were gathered at a far end of the area enjoying the sunshine, chatting, and puffing cigarettes. As I approached one of the standby limousines, a tousled man appeared from nowhere. Reaching into the car, he extracted and donned a jacket that had been folded over the front seat. Motioning me into the vehicle, the fellow climbed in and proceeded to drive me, in rather precarious fashion, to my destination, chatting amusingly all the while. His looks reminded me of someone, so I interrupted him long enough to comment that he bore a strong resemblance to the actor Danny Kaye.

"I wish!" he responded. "A lot of people tell me that I look like him. If I only had his talent and his dough."

As was customary in Palm Beach, when I exited the cab, the driver gave me a card with his phone number so that I might call to request transportation for the return to my hotel. Scribbling something across the card, he handed it to me. Having prearranged return transportation, and not wishing to litter the street, I slipped the reminder, unexamined, into a pocket of my jeans. Only the following morning, upon hearing that Mr. Kaye was, in fact, visiting south Florida, did I examine the card, across which my erstwhile driver had scrawled, "Have fun!" signing it with a flourish, "Danny Kaye."

My most extraordinary taxi-related experience occurred in Italy in the summer of 1950 during the Roman Catholic Church's first post World War II Holy Year celebrations. I was visiting Rome with a girlfriend when we hired a taxi to take us sightseeing in and around the Eternal City. Our driver was an elderly avuncular gentleman with an extravagant beard and kind eyes. At the end of our day of pride-filled, informative sightseeing, our guide, having taken a paternal interest in us, proposed that, at no cost whatsoever, he would arrange for us to have a "private" meeting with Pope Pius XII. (At the time, people were offering hundreds of dollars to bribe their way into any of the Pontiff's massive, though restricted, public audiences.) Our chauffeur instructed us on how to dress and what souvenirs we might bring for blessing by the pope.

The following morning, our mentor picked us up and drove us to the Vatican—not to the front entrance secured by flamboyant Swiss Guardsmen, but to an unobtrusive kitchen ingress located in a rear service court, where we were greeted by our cab driver's cousin, the Pope's valet. Led through a pantry and placed into a small elevator cum dumbwaiter, we were hoisted to an upper floor and released into the Pope's dressing room, a space crowded with elaborate robes, ceremonial accessories, and treasured relics. Ushered along a private hallway, we were deposited in an elegant, if bare, reception room already occupied by about a dozen respectfully attired devotees.

Presently, the white robed Pontiff entered, blessing all of us. I was situated first in the line of guests and he approached me with one hand extended. Shy and unsure of how to behave, I must have looked nervous.

"You're not a Catholic?" he smiled. "You are welcome to kiss my ring but if you think it may be too germ contaminated or if it offends your religion, there is no need."

I do not remember whether I kissed the large, gold-encased sapphire, but I do recall the Pope engaging me in lighthearted banter about college life in the United States. His English was fluent. I was clutching a number of rosaries intended as gifts for Catholic friends, when His Holiness, remarking that, upon entering the room, he had indeed blessed everyone and everything in the chamber, advised me that the eventual recipients of my rosaries would undoubtedly value them more if he held each piece in his own hands and blessed each item individually.

"Not to worry," he twinkled, "I won't steal anything, I'll return everything to you."

Unhurriedly, the Pope moved on, conversing with the remaining visitors in each one's native language. Although Pius was a tiny man, his personality and demeanor were so commanding he seemed to tower over everyone. After a final blessing, His Holiness departed, and we were dismissed.

13

I grew up accustomed to traveling. From the age of four I traveled extensively in the United States and overseas --- initially with my parents, then by myself and eventually with each of my two husbands. Significant memories were spawned in temporary domiciles. I always felt at home in transient lodgings and as an adult deliberately decorated my residences to resemble hotel suites or shipboard accommodations.

Following the Second World War and my father's death Mother and I spent prolonged summer vacations in Europe, principally in Paris. Having resided in Paris in order to obtain a divorce from her first husband, my mother had become enamored of France. An ardent Francophile and Parisian at heart, she wished to inculcate me with like-minded sentiment. Even our trusted travel agent was a Frenchman with offices in Paris and a mere subsidiary in New York.

Mother was quick to familiarize me with the habits and idiosyncrasies of her favorite city.

I spoke fluent French and blended in easily, making a number of staunch Parisian friends. I rarely felt like a tourist. Much of my clothing was purchased in Montmartre and I furnished my first New York City apartment with items acquired in Paris flea markets and wholesale venues.

Since most of Mother's relatives were habitual European travelers (and the post World War II dollar was exceptionally strong), it was not unusual for me to encounter aunts, uncles, great aunts and cousins while traveling abroad. In midsummer, strolling the Faubourg Staint-Honoré in Paris or Bond Street in London seemed as normal as browsing Manhattan's Fifth and Madison Avenues. I was as familiar with the morning newspaper *Le Figaro* as I was with the *New York Times*. My life in Paris was routine but, while I felt thoroughly at home there, I never became the Francophile for whom my mother wished.

For many years my Parisian home-away-from-home was the Hôtel Le Bristol on the Faubourg Saint Honoré. While traveling alone during my late twenties and early thirties I became a friend of the Jammets, the family that owned the hotel. They took especially attentive care of me; I was consistently pampered and almost intrusively protected. Even the hotel's elderly concierge took it upon himself to single me out, offering unsolicited, unctuous doses of grandfatherly advice while screening --- persistently approving or disapproving --- my visitors, especially my male escorts. He even vetted my taxi drivers.

It was my father --- an even more wide-ranging traveler and more prolific linguist than my mother --- who initially instilled in me my lifelong passion for travel. When I was only four, prior to taking mother and me to South America, he gave me sage advice: "When in a foreign country," he instructed, "never speak English unless it is literally a matter of life and death --- yours or someone else's. You can always make yourself understood by acting, drawing pictures, making exaggerated sounds and facial expressions. People will be patient and try to understand. If you speak English you will think in English, you will think like an American and you'll always be a tourist. You will never feel assimilated nor truly appreciate foreign cultures." Invaluable counsel.

Only rarely have I encountered difficulty in communicating. No matter when or where I have traveled I have never been disconcerted by language, even managing to master useful phrases in Finnish, Greek and Japanese.

While transitory residences customarily provided me with comfort, sundry accommodations were far from routine. Stranded unexpectedly in an overcrowded London and unable to find suitable lodging, the Dorchester Hotel (where I frequently resided) reluctantly, if graciously, provided me with sheets and a blanket and --- tactfully secreted by provisional folding screens --- allowed me to sleep, sequestered, on a couch in a remote corner of its elegant lobby. By contrast, years later --- when our longstanding reservation could not be honored by an inadvertently overbooked Claridge's --- my husband Joe and I were compensated with an upgrade to the hotel's ultra luxurious Royal Suite.

During a visit to India, Joe and I were housed in the sprawling, flamboyant palace apartment that had been occupied by Roger Moore during filming of the James Bond classic *Octopussy*. (A number of the movie's interiors had been filmed in the extravagant suite.) In contrast, some years earlier while exploring the upper Amazon by myself, I had been given "the very best" hotel room in Manaus, one equipped with wall hooks intended for my nonexistent personel hammock.

During a brief stay in Florence, Italy, the lobby of an innocuous guesthouse afforded me an education in the falsification of antiques. One morning, setting out later than usual, I noticed a housemaid, having discarded her dustpan, raise a portion of the reception room's ample sisal rug to sweep accumulated grime beneath it. "How improper; how lazy!" I thought, but it was none of my business so I continued on my way. A few days later I chanced upon a prominent local antiques dealer carefully removing the dust from beneath the textured floorcovering. As I watched, he stuffed the powder into a large sack, paying generously for the privilege. Pulverized by the traverse of many feet, the dirt's initial coarseness had been modified and "aged." Startled, I realized that the resulting accumulation was destined for application to the vendor's freshly manufactured "antiques" with the intent of disguising their true provenance.

The most disconcerting of my varied hotel experiences occurred when, as a single, potentially vulnerable young adult, I was obliged to share a hotel room --- and a bed --- with a stranger --- a formidable male stranger! Having disembarked an ocean liner in Rio de Janeiro following a trans Atlantic voyage, I was scheduled to continue to São Paulo. Due to bad weather, the departure of my connecting flight was delayed from mid afternoon until after midnight. A fellow steamship passenger, whom I knew only by sight, happened to be booked on the same plane. Prior to takeoff, we met in the airport lounge and grumbled together about the delay. Eventually, due to the pre-dawn hour of our arrival in São Paulo, the gentleman and I, encountering a paucity of available transportation, opted to share a taxi into town. When we arrived at a dimly lit, dormant hotel the sleepy-eyed desk clerk, reluctant to prepare a second guestroom and refusing to believe that two young people traveling together at such a questionable hour were strangers, was adamant that we share an accommodation. Too fatigued to prolong our protest and assured (incorrectly) that our room would have twin beds, we eventually, if reluctantly, acquiesced. Exhausted, the young man and I were forced to sleep cautiously alongside one another on a narrow double bed.

14

The following morning, that unlikely hotel stopover became even more improbable.

We were awakened by resounding noise reverberating from somewhere outside our room. It sounded as though a few men were simultaneously laughing and arguing with one another. When my roommate and I looked into the hall, we saw an assortment of scruffy, military-fatigue garbed men conversing and occasionally struggling with one another. A man who seemed to be in control of the unruly group might have been attractive had he not appeared dirty and disheveled. His face was familiar from the news media. I recognized him immediately. The slovenly man was Cuba's newly inaugurated Prime Minister, Fidel Castro. What a crude and unappealing first impression!

With Fidel's help, the men—who included Che Guevara—were attempting to corral and control a number of squawking chickens—fowl presumably intended to insure the men a safe, self-prepared, non-contaminated dinner. Noticing me, Castro nodded in my direction, smiled, and turned away, continuing to pursue the troublesome birds. The hallway was a noisy mess. The customarily decorous hotel seemed to have disintegrated into a disheveled motel. I packed my bags immediately and evacuated.

When reflecting upon memorable events of one's lifetime, one may recall where one was when one became aware of notable occurrences. Because I traveled extensively, I was frequently away from home. Some of my recollections may have been significant, others merely selective.

In Brazil, aside from my encounter with Castro, I became acquainted with the introduction of Salk's polio vaccine, the Israeli capture of Adolf Eichmann, Yuri Gagarin's breakthrough globe-circling space flight, Robert Kennedy's assassination, and the contentious Army-McCarthy hearings (during which, my Brazilian families both suggested that it might be unwise—even unsafe—for me to return to the United States).

In Paris, riveted to my hotel's television set, I watched Neil Armstrong descend onto the surface of the moon and O. J. Simpson in his white Ford Bronco fleeing authorities following the murder of his wife. I was in France when the newspaper, *Le Figaro,* informed me of Marilyn Monroe's suspicious death, of Grace Kelly's fatal accident, of Jacqueline Kennedy's demise. In mid-ocean, watching television on board the *SS France,* I watched President Nixon resign from office. I learned about the tragedies of 9/11 while in a hospital recovering from heart bypass surgery.

Of necessity, as one ages and acquires new companions, newsworthy recollections can connect retirees to one another. Shared memories may invoke a sense of generational compatibility and security in having mutually encountered familiar events and experiences. There may be compatibility and comfort in the communal.

15

When speaking a foreign language, as I often did, misinterpreting and misusing similar sounding words was not uncommon. Despite a natural gift for languages, and having been raised to feel comfortable communicating in unfamiliar vernaculars, I experienced a number of memorable faux pas.

One of those blunders occurred in a small village in the backcountry of Brazil. Wishing to have my hair washed and set, I found the town's only so-called beauty parlor. The rather grungy establishment was located at one end of a dusty, unpaved, central square, in the middle of which was an ancient pump that supplied the entire neighborhood with running water.

In the 1950s, sophisticated city hairdressers frequently employed beer as a setting lotion. When the rudimentary beauty shop's proprietor was about to go outside to fetch water for my shampoo, I asked if she would please set my hair with beer. She looked at me rather strangely and asked if I was sure that was what I wanted; it seemed rather odd to her.

"Yes," I assured her, that was what I preferred.

Shrugging her shoulders in condescending disbelief and disapproval, she strolled to a nearby café, returning with a bulky, sweating carton, the creamy, chilled, but melting contents of which she reluctantly poured over my hair and massaged onto my freshly washed scalp. Instead of *cerveja* (beer), I had politely but firmly requested similar-sounding *sorvete* (ice cream).

I have always found it considerably more difficult to understand a less familiar vocabulary when communicating by telephone. One tranquil weekend morning, when I was first living in São Paulo and still perfecting my Portuguese, I experienced an embarrassing misunderstanding. Conversing with one of my Brazilian "uncles," I inquired after his mother (who lived in another city and, believed to be terminally ill, was failing fast). I was extremely fond of the old lady, who was like a second grandmother to me. To my surprise and delight, I understood *tio* (uncle) Clemente to say that "*ella melhorou* (she got better)." Prior to hanging up, I told him effusively how pleased I was to hear such good news. Later that day, as was my custom on casual Sunday afternoons, I attended the weekly family get-together at *tio* Clemente's home. When I arrived in my bubbly, obviously upbeat mood, I was startled to see most of the family grim faced and dressed in black. Suddenly I realized that what I thought I had heard, "*ella melhorou* (she improved)," had actually been "*ella morreu* (she died)."

Recently, while reminiscing, one of my elderly neighbors, reflecting upon her happy childhood as the daughter of European parents who owned and operated a Chinese restaurant in south Florida, recalled that both the chef and the manager of the establishment had been Chinese and conversed with one another in their native language. Both employees were consistently playful and kind, always calling my friend *chónghài*, a pet name she assumed could be translated affectionately as "honey," "cutie," or some similar complementary appellation. Eventually, when one of her adult grandchildren began to study Chinese, my neighbor sought the precise definition of *chónghài*, only to learn that it was a term for "pest."

Vacationing in Mexico, a bachelor friend of mine became yet another victim of lingual misuse. With two male friends, David left a nightclub well after midnight. Hungry, the trio searched for someplace where they might obtain a light repast. Unsuccessful, the men eventually stopped an elderly stranger and, attempting to communicate in spontaneously devised artificial Spanish, asked the fellow if he happened to know where they might obtain some hot food at that dubious pre-dawn hour. The gentleman smiled, nodded eagerly, disappeared for a moment, and returned with three provocatively dressed young women, gaudy prostitutes. Seeking an all-night eatery in their presumptuous but inadequate and ill-pronounced attempt to Latinize the word for kitchen, the men had asked for a *cochina* (a woman's private parts) rather than a *cucina* (a kitchen).

Despite occasional inconvenience, languages, passports and visas have neither defined nor restricted me. While my principle residence has always been in the United States, I have felt equally at home in foreign countries.

Like my father and my second husband, I am customarily at ease in less familiar surroundings. I am comfortable with contrasting, potentially conflicting, ideas and ideologies. Because of our experiences, contacts, and dispositions, rather than our politics or political affiliations, my father, my husband, and I were all offered enviable diplomatic assignments, posts that, regrettably, each of us felt obliged to decline.

Three decades apart, my father and my husband were offered the position of United States Ambassador to Brazil. Reluctantly, primarily for family and financial reasons, both turned down the assignment.

During the 1960s, concurrent with the régime of French Prime Minister Charles de Gaulle, I was residing in Brazil and dating a promising Carioca career diplomat. To my surprise, the Brazilian Foreign Minister sought me out. Doggedly urging me to marry his young protégé, he assured me that if Mauricio and I were to wed, with me as an ideal helpmate and hostess, my spouse would become Brazil's next ambassador to France. It was a promise. Although both flattered and intrigued by the prospect of diplomatic life and Parisian residency, I was not sufficiently attracted to the prospective groom to consider the union. Moreover, because I harbored a political and philosophical dislike and distrust of de Gaulle, the prospect of having to socialize and ingratiate myself with him held scant appeal.

16

According to their composers, I have had two songs, one extremely popular, the other not particularly successful, dedicated to me.

Early in our marriage my first husband, composer and lyricist Edward Kean, wrote and recorded a tune entitled *The Only Love*, which he dedicated to me. It had a pretty melody and pleasantly romantic lyrics, but the vocalist who recorded the demo was not sufficiently well known and, although a number of radio disc jockeys aired it, the piece was never seriously nor adequately promoted.

Some years earlier I had been told that a new French melody was being dedicated to me. That song became extremely popular, not merely throughout Europe, but worldwide. Notable renditions were recorded by twenty-eight artists including Yves Montand, Jean Sablon, Barbra Streisand and Frank Sinatra. The song's composer was a flirtatious gentleman whom I encountered during a vacation in Switzerland. Seeking a midafternoon snack while staying at Badrutt's Palace Hotel in St. Moritz, I wandered into the hotel's semi-deserted lobby, arriving somewhat prior to the commencement of high tea. The large space was empty except for a few waiters preparing tables for the afternoon get-together and a gentleman who was seated at the grand piano, playing softly. Since there were no other guests present, the entertainer invited me to join him on the piano bench and chat with him while he rehearsed. One of the tunes, unfamiliar to me, was a little wistful but extremely catchy and appealing. Although the musician was performing a variety of popular songs, he kept replaying the piece that intrigued me.

"What a lovely melody! What is it?" I inquired.

"It's my newest composition," he replied, "it's called *Clopin Clopant;* the English version will be called *Comme Ci Comme Ca.*" Smiling indulgently he continued, "Since I've just finished writing it and you like it so much the song is yours; I dedicate it to you."

More than sixty years later, the melody is still being performed. When I hear it I wonder to how many additional young women the flirtatious composer dedicated *my* tune.

17

From the time that I began drawing sketches as a toddler I have always been immersed in the art world; I am most content when creating something --- anything --- visually, emotionally and/or intellectually pleasing. I have enjoyed writing, drawing, painting, working with clay, knitting, crocheting, designing both clothing and interiors, viewing and collecting works of art, attending concerts, opera and the theater.

I have always loved the theater. Throughout high school and college I designed and helped execute scenery and costumes for theatrical productions. I would have liked to make stagecraft my career but my parents, always striving for whatever seemed most esteemed, discouraged me. "Rather than designing artificial, temporary spaces, create permanent, functional ones," they insisted. "Become a respected architect, rather than an obscure set designer."

In the early 1950s women in my environment were rarely considered viable architects --- only potential draft persons. Not interested in confronting and combating a challenge, I demurred.

Considerably later in life, I became an interior designer with an instinctively theatrical agenda. Consciously and conscientiously I treated my interiors as stage sets. I designed environments that I deemed complimentary to the personalities and activities each space was destined to encompass. So long as the quality and execution of the rooms I designed were satisfactory, I did not personally have to like their appearance; I was not going to live in the interiors, my clients were. One of my most successful projects was for a Brazilian family whose taste was diametrically opposed to mine. Recognizing their likes and dislikes I filled their residence with quality items that I personally detested. They adored the result and enthusiastically recommended me to other potential clients.

Since early adulthood many of my friends and acquaintances have been professional artists. Although I did not encounter a domestic television set until after the Second World War, a considerable number of my acquaintances were involved in television and the performing arts.

My initial exposure to a privately owned television occurred during a visit to my elderly Great Aunt Leah. In her elegant Fifth Avenue apartment overlooking Central Park a small stand surrounded by museum quality old master paintings supported a sizable wooden box with a miniscule glass screen. The screen was even smaller than the photographs I could snap with my new Kodak Brownie camera but miraculously the contraption's enticing, black and white images were actually moving! The set had been a recent gift to my aunt from her gadget-enamored son George who had failed to consider that there would be nothing appealing for his aging, prim and very docile mother to watch. In essence, there were only test patterns and an increasingly popular series of shows featuring a controversial professional wrestler named Gorgeous George --- hardly appropriate entertainment for a sheltered and timid old lady.

Gorgeous George was a charismatic character whose pre-fight antics and in-fight cheating deliberately antagonized audiences. Detesting him, fans booed enthusiastically. Although an adept competitor, George brazenly cheated at every opportunity, blatantly drawing attention to his offences. A natural showman, George's approach and entry into the ring usually lasted longer than the fights that followed. Accompanied by a tuxedoed valet scattering rose petals and spraying Channel No. 5 "disinfectant" around him, wrapped in flamboyant, sequin embellished robes, George would enter the arena to the strains of *Pomp and Circumstance*. Affecting a specious effeminate persona, he would enhance his long blond curls with golden bobby pins that he withdrew and tossed into the audience as souvenirs. To my amazement, captivated by this dynamic bravura, my frail, wizened, little aunt would sit, transfixed, in her favorite wing chair punching the air violently with clenched fists and grunting sympathetically.

Eventually, the demeanor of young Cassius Clay, the panache of Liberace and the audacious grandstanding of Donald Trump were all inspired by George's pattern of outrageous antics, his philosophy of self-promotion, his conviction that it was unimportant whether the public loved you or hated you so long as they were mindful of you.

Due to scant competition during the early days of television the popularity of wrestling matches --- especially presentations as colorful and controversial as Gorgeous George's --- burgeoned. His series became the first television broadcast to earn a profit. During the early 1950s the self-aggrandizing villain --- the highest paid athlete in the world --- was credited with motivating and maximizing the purchase of television sets.

Television sales were further inspired by *Texaco Star Theater*, a vaudeville show hosted by comedian Milton Berle (or Uncle Miltie as he was affectionately known). In the autumn of 1948, shortly after I settled into collegiate life at Temple University in suburban Philadelphia, I was invited to the home of a prominent local family, casual acquaintances of my parents, to be introduced to a few potentially compatible (and possibly dateable) young Philadelphians. By the time I arrived the entire party had gathered around a tiny television set. *Texaco Star Theater* was just commencing. I was waved into the darkened room, pointed to a seat and motioned not to speak. By the time the television show concluded and lamps had been relit, it was dormitory curfew time for me and I had to rush off without being introduced to any of my prospective new friends. That was the impact, the power, of early television at a time when set ownership was still restricted to the homes of a privileged few.

As time passed, television and the people who created its magic became a routine part of my life. My favorite cousin, Jane, married William Bratter a senior partner in the law firm Marshall, Bratter, Greene, Alison and Tucker. Bill, who headed the firm's entertainment division, was a founding member of The National Academy of Television Arts and Sciences (grantor of the Emmy Awards). In addition to prominent game show producers Goodson and Todman, clients with whom Bill socialized included numerous emerging celebrates. Following the launch of *The Gary Moore Show* Bill, who worked closely with Gary, was instrumental in both the hiring and the molding of a novice Carol Burnett.

A frequent guest at the Bratters' dinner parties, I became acquainted with, among others, Arlene Frances, Kitty Carlisle, Bill Cullen, Bess Myerson, Bennett Cerf (who attempted, unsuccessfully, to encourage me to become a professional author), and Merv Griffin (with whom I attended Bill Bratter's unexpected, remarkably youthful funeral). Early on, Gary Moore and his wife Nell became good friends of mine.

Another cousin, Louise, married Michael Dann, the esteemed programmer for NBC and, subsequently, for CBS. Mike was a tough, no-nonsense executive who consistently kept whichever network employed him rated number one in the competitive rankings. Among the many shows for which Mike was responsible over the years were *Green Acres, Mission Impossible, The Mary Tyler Moore Show, The Carol Burnett Show, Hawaii Five-O* and *60 Minutes*. He was also responsible for hiring --- and much later firing --- the Smothers

Brothers. A valued consultant to broadcasters around the world, Mike was also involved in the planning of Disney's Epcot Center.

At a time when Mike was serving as consultant to the British Broadcasting System, I happened to mention that I was attempting to write an historical novel about Elizabeth Patterson Bonaparte, the American wife of Napoleon's youngest brother Jérôme. Betsy had led a life of intrigue and glamour and her nineteenth century adventures seemed to parallel and fore-shadow those of an equally controversial fellow Baltimorean, the Duchess of Windsor. (Unlike the duchess, Betsy bore a son and his son, Napoleon's great-nephew Charles Joseph Bonaparte, United States Attorney General under Theodore Roosevelt, founded the FBI.) Because Betsy was beautiful and clever but not particularly likeable, I was finding it difficult to turn her story into an appealing narrative yet I could envision her adventures as a riveting and visually splendid television series in the BBC/PBS tradition. Mike agreed and suggested that I write a treatment for him to submit to the gurus of *Masterpiece Theater*. Timid and unsure of myself as a potential playwright, I never followed through.

Watching television may rekindle recollections of the half-forgot-ten. Prior to viewing a segment of *Antiques Roadshow* on Public Television I had been unaware that Howard Carter, the Egyptologist who discovered Tutankhamen's tomb, had been a gifted watercolorist. Watching as three of his paintings were appraised on TV, I visualized my wedding to Joseph Jones. The ceremony had taken place in the pine-scented Adirondack mountain home of Carter's nephew, Theodore. Ted, wearing his family tartan, had not only been our host, but our principal witness. The memory also reminded me that the sponsor of Howard Carter's Egyptian forays had been Lord Carnarvon at whose home, Highclere Castle, I had been a guest long before it served as a principal location for the British television series *Downton Abby*.

My first husband, Edward Kean, was the creator --- scriptwriter, composer and lyricist --- of the 1950s-1960s children's television classic, *Howdy Doody*. As such, Ed was at least partially responsible for advancing the careers of Robert Goulet and William Shatner, casting each of them as a principal character in the Canadian version of the show. By firing Bob Keeshan from his role as Clarabell the Clown on the *Howdy Doody Show* Ed inadvertently enabled creation of the immensely successful, competitive children's program *Captain Kangaroo* and the providential career of Captain Kangaroo himself. In addition, composing and arranging music for a young nightclub vocalist at the outset of a multi-facetted career, Ed abetted the initial success of then fledgling band singer Merv Griffin.

In midlife I myself became involved in television, going to work as an assistant consumer advocate-consultant at WNEW-TV, New York's Channel 5 Metromedia station. Of all my varied occupations, that employment was my favorite. I enjoyed discovering and then wielding the power of the press. I found satisfaction and reward in helping the abused, advising and educating the unwary. I enjoyed the energy and excitement of the newsroom. As an added bonus, I delighted in associating with the likes of award-winning correspondent Gabe Pressman (and attending his family's glug enhanced Christmas parties); conversing with talk show host David Susskind; associating with Jim Henson, Frank Oz and the Muppets. I enjoyed being able to chat with celebrities like David Frost, Henry Kissinger and Bing Crosby.

18

After relocating to Florida, I was invited to attend and participate in the broadcast of a local primetime newscast. More than fifty years had elapsed since I worked in the Metromedia newsroom in Manhattan. Although the vast changes in technique and technology were no surprise, they were nonetheless impressive. During the 1960s, the din when one entered a newsroom was deafening. Adding to the cacophony of typewriters, ringing telephones, and reporters' resonant cursing were the ubiquitous ticker-tape machines (so named because of the sound they made). Distracting appliances, the devices continuously transmitted breaking news (significant or not) to attentive correspondents.

The Florida newsroom, with its virtually silent monitors, computers, control panels, and hush-voiced personnel, was whisper-quiet, a welcome antithesis to my previous milieu. Compared to the former frenetic environment, the updated venue generated an illusion of tranquility, its improved efficiency exemplified by the replacement of hurriedly scrawled, handheld cue cards with more legible computer-generated prompts displayed across stable monitors.

The transformation brought to mind another evolution in communication. I visualized the wooden telephones of my childhood, instruments that had to be cranked before usage. They were succeeded by so-called "trumpet" phones, devices that stood upright on a side table or hung, box-like, on a wall, activated and deactivated by manipulating tubular earpieces stored on protruding metal hooks.

As a youngster, my family's summer residence was connected to a party line—one ring for us, two or three for additional subscribers—with the predictable inconvenience of listening to or inadvertently interrupting overlapping conversations.

When I was still quite young, the telephone was reconfigured into a squat rectangular instrument. The previously separated speaker and earpiece were combined into a single, hand-held device. Because dials were rather stiff, in order to protect her manicure when placing a call, my mother would employ the blunt end of a pencil. Hotels and businesses had large, desk-like switchboards that functioned with long cables manipulated by operators wearing microphones and earphones.

Eventually, quadrangular black phones shrank in size, were remodeled into an oval configuration, manufactured in various colors, and dubbed "princess phones."

When I graduated college, although push buttons had begun to replace dials, Call Waiting, Caller ID, and electronic answering machines were still nonexistent. Eventually, cordless telephones became available, as did portable cell phones, forerunners of today's ubiquitous "Smart Phones."

Initially a luxury, telephones have become a necessity. Continuously evolving, the apparatus has not merely kept pace with, but has contributed to, the world's ongoing renovation.

19

Technical advancements, while welcome, do not necessarily sponsor unmitigated improvement. Some of the presumed deficiencies and inefficiencies of my childhood were actually enriching, even beneficial. Requisite additional mental and emotional effort often outweighed today's comparative passivity.

Prior to Instant Messaging, Twitter, Facebook, and other social media, before the continuous accessibility of television and computer games, one was forced to be more self-reliant, more inventive. Seeking enlightenment and entertainment from books, radio, and newspapers, we were obliged to become creatively involved.

When home entertainment was primarily confined to radio, rather than merely looking at an image on a television screen, we were obliged to be inventive, to visualize the appearance of a news item, a soap opera, or a philharmonic concert. We had to imagine what the performers, their costumes, environment, and activities looked like. Participation and creativity were requisite. Supplemental input was essential; the mind was activated.

There was also less requisite for us to be wary.

A few years ago, I received a telephone call from my stepdaughter, Patricia, that aroused my suspicions. While pursuing her interest in genealogy, a woman had contacted Pat, claiming to be related to me on my mother's side of the family. The caller had requested my e-mail address or, better yet, my telephone number. Suspecting a scam, Pat declined the request, but offered to relay the woman's assertions and her e-mail address; if interested, I could contact the inquisitor.

Thanks to my family-factual mother and grandmother, I believed I could account for all of my maternal relatives and assumed the inquirer must be a fraud. Nevertheless, included in the woman's message was an interesting assertion: she claimed that my maternal grandfather, who always professed to be from Germany, had actually been Polish.

Although fluent in German, a language he refused to speak—asserting that if he had liked Germany he would have remained there—my grandfather (who died before I was born) had, in fact, relocated to the United States from a section of Poland that, at the time he emigrated, had been controlled by Russia.

Because, in the 1800s, immigrant Jews from Poland were looked down upon and treated as intellectually and socially inferior by their European counterparts, Hyman Cohen had concealed his true identity, even from his unsuspecting offspring. Quite by chance, in midlife, I stumbled across the truth but kept the discovery to myself. How and what did the inquiring stranger know? Just possibly, she and I might be related!

The interrogator's name was Bonnie, and she lived in Minnesota. Curiosity aroused, I contacted her and, upon conferring, determined that we were, indeed, distant cousins. My grandfather, Hyman Cohen, and Bonnie's great-grandfather, Joseph Cohen, had been brothers. In addition, the men had a sister, Ruchla, whose great-granddaughter, Barbara, born and bred in Florida, lived only a few miles from my current residence.

Exchanging information, I remembered that at the beginning of the Second World War, my mother's family had been informed, evidently incorrectly, that all relatives still residing in Europe (including Bonnie's branch of the family) had been exterminated by the Nazis. In actual fact, Bonnie's then young grandfather, great-uncle, and great-aunt had survived and escaped. Eventually reaching the United States, each had established a multi-generational American family.

Bonnie also mentioned Herbert Saul, another European relative; a refugee who had settled briefly in Brooklyn before relocating to Minnesota. I had encountered Saul on a number of occasions and liked him. Bonnie remembered him, our mutual cousin, as the genial man who had facilitated her family's settlement in the Midwest.

Safety, secrecy, and accuracy aside, the convenience and omnipresence of cell phones have transformed our usage of time and the conduct of interpersonal relationships. Worldwide twenty-four-hour accessibility can foster emotional stress and physical exhaustion. The turning of day into night and night into day allows little or no rest for the weary and overburdened. Increasingly, there is less time for quiet contemplation, less time to relax and revive. Continuous tension and sleep deprivation challenge physical health, alertness, sound judgment, and emotional stability. Social intercourse is being revised. Text messages are replacing vocal exchanges. Acronyms replace whole words and phrases. Traditional grammatical correctness is becoming obsolete. Virtual reality is replacing face-to-face encounters. With its permissive anonymity, social media allows aggressive confrontation, enabling the brash, all too often dire, consequences of bullying.

Widespread addiction to the convenience, information, entertainment, and distraction of the internet, can corrode social interaction, particularly among today's youth. How does a child learn to socialize if his attention is consistently concentrated upon and satisfied by a device, rather than by other human beings? Increasingly, physical isolation and self-absorption encourage narcissism, blind trust, misinterpretation, and misunderstandings. Disregard for feelings and potential consequences abounds.

All too often, we embrace escapism, rather than ameliorate what needs to be escaped from. Patience and sympathetic understanding have, too often, become virtues of the past. Increasingly, the emphasis is on the *I* rather than the *we*, on the *me* rather than the *us*. We have become selfish and self-absorbed. Desensitized, our baser emotions, formerly controlled, or at least concealed, are not only displayed but tolerated. Violent anger, brutality, bullying, and road rage are proliferating, even accepted as normal. Guns, far too easily attainable, settle far too many grievances.

Despite my skepticism, reservations, and resistance, I am aware that the internet can have a positive effect, even upon reluctant users like myself. Like so much in life, progress can be a mixed blessing. While society and social intercourse may be slow to adapt to advancing technology, new devices, and their usage enable much that is welcome and worthwhile. In addition to offering useful gadgetry, unlimited instant information, protective pronouncements, and welcome entertainment, interactive programs—especially those with visual capabilities—provide otherwise inaccessible instructors, distant friends, and scattered families with more satisfying interaction. Relationships between physically remote individuals are enabled and enhanced.

Detached by both age and necessity from the need to contemporize, I cling contentedly to certain comforts of the past, to what I consider to have been a relatively calmer, more relaxed lifestyle.

Cautiously, I explore, even embrace, and enjoy, sundry innovations. Despite my reticence, thanks to technical advances, my world is changing. While my environment is being streamlined, it is simultaneously becoming more enigmatic. In some ways, my milieu seems less complicated; in other ways, it seems considerably more complex.

20

For me, age has become erroneous. Without children of my own, I tend to entertain a skewed sense of time. Confounding my concept of time is the realization that the children of my contemporaries (whom I have not seen in many a year and still picture as youngsters) are retirees, grandparents, even great-grandparents. I am always surprised by the frequency of obituaries that portray people younger than myself. Although I am well into the stage of life where death is predictable, even anticipated, I feel remote from its imminence. Eulogies in the newspaper inspire me to regard myself as fortunate, healthy, and young. I sense that, consistent with my long life, I have been granted a bonus, an opportunity to serve, to give back, to be thankful.

Due to their increasing scarcity, as time passes, surviving lifelong acquaintances become more cherished and appealing, not merely because they share memories of parents, deceased spouses, and mutual friends, but because they can identify with meaningful events and innovations, with obsolete circumstances, and the once familiar, if currently outmoded, paraphernalia of previous decades.

I marvel at how significantly the world has changed. Former countries have disappeared; new nations have risen. Globalism is replacing intimacy.

The mid-twentieth century's seemingly casual and congenial pace of life has given way to a more detached, more impersonal environment. In both action and interaction, machines are displacing humans. Automation and a surfeit of too frequently inaccurate and deceptive information have begun to dominate our planet. Mechanized exchanges are replacing the intimacy and sensitivity of face-to-face encounters.

The joys and frustrations of shopping are being revised. Small mom-and-pop shops, large department stores, and national chains are giving way to internet acquisition. The days of convivial marketing, when my mother and grandmother would venture from butcher to greengrocer to bakery chatting familiarly with shop owners while sampling potential purchases, have been supplanted by one-stop shopping in copious supermarkets where the availability of fresh produce from around the world has eradicated the seasonal restrictions of yesteryear.

The rudimentary iceboxes of my early childhood have been supplanted by ever-evolving refrigerators, appliances that offer electronic options, including internet access and the ability to photograph contents and create marketing lists. Gas stoves have been supplemented by electronic and induction cooktops. Microwave ovens, introduced in 1965, were slow to gain acceptance and did not become popular until the 1980s. Today, a state-of-the-art microwave can calculate the weight of meat inserted into it, the time and temperature required to cook that meat, and then prepare the meat accordingly. Light bulbs have gone from short-lived and power-hungry to seemingly everlasting and energy-efficient. Transportation continues to contemporize. The crank primed automobiles of my youth have evolved into self-driving vehicles. Coal-fed locomotives have been supplanted by high-speed bullet trains. Single engine, parachute equipped aircraft have been supplanted by huge jetliners, supersonic transport, and space travel. Steam-powered ocean liners have been supplemented by nuclear vessels.

Wristwatches that required winding and simply told time are evolving into timepieces that communicate with the world, illuminating—even determining—a wearer's health and use of time. Abbreviated texting is lessening the eloquence and elegance of letter writing. Computerization and automation—even when dependent upon challenging learning curves—are reinventing the world.

21

Much of what we currently take for granted was nonexistent, unused, or unfamiliar when we were youngsters. Much of what we considered routine is incomprehensible to twenty-first-century adolescents who have never seen and have no concept of ticker tape or telegrams, lick-necessitating postage stamps, human-operated telephone switchboards, cumbersome telephone directories, and rotary telephones. Many are unfamiliar with film cameras and film that took a week to develop, reel-to-reel tape recorders, floppy discs, and the need for whiteout with non-self-correcting manual typewriters. For many, cursive script, library card catalogs, and slide rules are unfamiliar and obsolete. Even answering machines and public payphones are regarded as conveniences of the past by youths who cannot conceive of a world without universal, instantaneous, portable communication.

The internet is reforming our lives, from how we relate to one another to how we apportion our time. The tempo and demeanor of our existence are being transformed. The distinction between daytime and nighttime activities has become far less pronounced. Television no longer ceases to broadcast during the wee hours, transmitting only immobile channel logos overnight. It is no longer preferable to place long-distance telephone calls after dark in order to take advantage of reduced rates.

Worldwide instant communication and ever-advancing techniques offering explicit information on virtually everything have become purveyors of accidental and deliberate disinformation. All too often, the ability to distinguish between the accurate and the inaccurate has become obscure. As a result, I have become universally suspicious—a skeptic, a wary and reluctant utilizer of the internet. With access to everything, there is assurance of nothing. By extension, I have become distrustful of my peers. I no longer believe in the veracity of anyone or anything at first encounter. I am reluctant to transact business or transmit personal information online. I confide as little about my life, my possessions, and myself as possible. A fiercely private person, I guard my privacy ferociously, albeit with increasing difficulty.

Safety, secrecy, and accuracy aside, the universality of cell phones is transforming the usage of time and the conduct of interpersonal relationships. Worldwide twenty-four-hour accessibility can foster emotional stress and physical exhaustion. The turning of day into night and night into day allows little or no rest for the weary and overburdened. Increasingly, there is less time for quiet contemplation, less time to relax, and revive. Tension and sleep deprivation challenge physical health, alertness, sound judgment, and emotional stability. Social intercourse is being revised. Text messaging is replacing vocal exchanges. Acronyms are replacing whole words and phrases. Traditional grammatical correctness is becoming obsolete. Virtual reality is replacing face-to-face encounters. Social media, with its permissive anonymity, allows aggressive confrontation, enabling the brash, all too often dire, consequences of bullying.

With widespread addiction to the convenience, information, entertainment, and distractions of the internet, social interaction—particularly among today's youth—is being corroded. How does a child learn to socialize if his attention is consistently concentrated upon and satisfied by a device rather than by other human beings? Increasingly, physical isolation and self-absorption encourage narcissism, blind trust, misinterpretation, and misunderstandings. Disregard for feelings and eventualities abounds. All too often, we embrace escapism, rather than ameliorate what needs to be escaped from. Patience and sympathetic understanding have too often become virtues of the past. Increasingly, emphasis is on the *I* rather than the *we*, on the *me* rather than the *us*. We have become selfish and self-absorbed. Desensitized, our baser emotions, formerly controlled or at least concealed, are not only displayed but tolerated, even encouraged. Anger, brutality, bullying, and road rage are proliferating and, all too often, being accepted as normal.

Nevertheless, while society is slow to adapt emotionally to advancing technology, new devices and their usage enable much that is welcome and worthwhile. In addition to providing useful gadgetry, instant information, protective pronouncements, welcome entertainment, and facilitated shopping, interactive programs—especially those with visual capabilities—bring far-flung friends and physically scattered families into closer, more frequent, and more satisfying communication. Relationships between geographically remote individuals, interaction between aging relatives and their far-flung descendants are being enhanced, facilitated, and enriched.

Age is insignificant. Even toddlers may be addicted to the internet. Shortly before Thanksgiving, I chanced to overhear a neighbor's visiting great-grandchild proudly advise his grandmother that he was all grown up and no longer believed in Santa Claus. Following his declaration, the youngster requested a pencil and some notepaper and, when asked to whom he wished to write, replied: "to Santa because I don't want to hurt his feelings."

Detached by both age and necessity from the need to contemporize, I cling contentedly to comforts of the past, to what I consider to have been a relatively calmer, more relaxed lifestyle. Even so, I cautiously explore, even embrace and enjoy, sundry innovations. Despite my reluctance, thanks to technical advances, my world is changing. While my environment is being streamlined, it is simultaneously becoming more enigmatic. In some ways, my world seems less complicated; in other ways, it seems considerably more complex.

22

Some years ago, wishing to relax while improving my figure, I selected a fashionable spa in south Florida as my habitual retreat between trips to Europe and Brazil. Memories of Palmaire include casual chats with a rather raunchy Elizabeth Taylor, and avoiding a young, newly successful Billy Joel who, having requested anonymity, was devastated when fellow guests, out of consideration for his privacy, pretended not to recognize him. I enjoyed watching Goldie Hawn care for her newborn daughter and observing Douglas Fairbanks, Jr., during visits with his health-reinforcing wife.

At Palmaire, I fraternized with an assortment of engaging, less recognizable fellow patrons, including real estate tycoons, antique dealers, glamorous mistresses, trophy spouses, and Mafia wives.

An older couple I met there became lifelong friends. About to purchase a Chagall lithograph to add to their art collection, they asked me, as a practicing fine arts consultant, to assess the piece. Finding both the print and its signature suspect, I advised against the acquisition, presumably saving the couple a considerable amount of money.

In 1979, during a Christmastime visit to the spa, I became friendly with Patricia, a fellow guest with whom I dined regularly. One afternoon, while sharing a relaxed lunch, Pat was summoned to the telephone. When she returned, her face was ashen; she was visibly shaken.

Tears welling in her eyes, Pat cried, "An ambulance has rushed my best friend to the hospital in a potentially irreversible coma. I've been afraid she was overly depressed and taking too much medication--but this? A few weeks ago--we thought it was an accident--she took an overdose of pills but was resuscitated. She's hypoglycemic, and now it appears she has taken a potentially lethal injection of insulin. I've tried so hard to help her deal with alcohol, drugs, and her personal demons, apparently to no avail. I've got to fly back to Rhode Island to see if there's anything I can do for her or her poor husband."

Although Patricia returned north, there was nothing she or anyone else could do to restore Sunny von Bülow's health. Comatose, von Bülou survived in a vegetative state for an additional twenty-eight years.

Although my fellow guest's spontaneous reaction to her friend's predicament was neither suspicious nor accusative, Sonny's husband Claus was charged with attempting to murder his wife. A high profile trial ensued. Convicted, Claus was subsequently vindicated on appeal, defended in part by a colorful young lawyer named Alan Dershowitz and vouched for by such character witnesses as Truman Capote and other high-profile members of café society. As recounted by Dershowitz in his best-selling book *Reversal of Fortune*, the case became the basis of an Oscar-winning film starring Jeremy Irons and Glenn Close.

After his exoneration, as fellow art lovers and auction addicts who frequently encountered one another, von Bülou and I became nodding acquaintances. He was always a gentleman, courteous, cordial, unpretentious, but slightly aloof.

23

On a November afternoon in 1965, I joined next-door neighbors for an impromptu trip to the Sears-Roebuck establishment in Queens. We were inspired to make the journey by advertisements advising that Vincent Price would be visiting the store that afternoon, introducing the Vincent Price Collection of Fine Art that the store would be offering for sale.

Although recognized worldwide as an accomplished actor acclaimed for his myriad performances on both stage and screen, unknown to the general public, Price was admired in fine arts circles as a disciplined collector and true connoisseur. Educated at Yale University and overseas, a former gallery owner and lecturer, Price had been employed by Sears to establish and oversee their attempt to supply affordable art to the masses. The actor acquired many of the offerings he assembled directly from prominent living artists who were his personal friends.

Upon reaching the store, my companions and I encountered a surprisingly generous assortment of works by an impressive variety of illustrators, all attractively framed and guaranteed to be authentic. Works we admired included pieces by Rembrandt van Rijn, Pablo Picasso, Salvador Dali, Andrew Wyeth, and Norman Rockwell. We looked around leisurely, genuinely admiring many of the offerings. Artworks priced from ten dollars to three thousand dollars could be purchased for as little as five dollars down with payments of five dollars each month thereafter. During its nine years of existence, the department sold more than fifty thousand pieces.

Tempted to purchase a number of items, I finally settled on a colorful lithograph from Chagall's *Daphnis and Chloe Suite*. The cost was negligible, and--to my surprise and pleasure--it was the articulate, urbane Mr. Price himself who waited on me.

My companions also bought a few items, and, as dusk fell, it was time to return to Manhattan. Joining the rush hour traffic, we left for home. It was just past five o'clock. By five-thirty, the sky had turned crimson, streaked with sunset. Suddenly, lights along the highway began to flicker and die. The skyline of Manhattan looming to the west of us went dark. Until the moon rose, the only illumination came from the headlights and taillights of hindered vehicles. A massive electrical outage stretched across some eighty thousand square miles of central Canada and the northeastern United States. The blackout affected thirty million people and lasted far into the night. A profusion of spur-of-the-moment volunteers came to aid victims. The predicament seemed to bring out the best in normally apathetic New Yorkers. Surprisingly, there was little, if any, looting.

Eventually, safe but exhausted, my companions and I reached our pitch-dark residence. Stowing our cumbersome purchases safely in a down-stairs locker, clutching borrowed flashlights, and halting intermittently to catch our breath, we ascended the building's indoor fire stairs to our adjoining apartments on the eleventh floor.

Sometimes the process of acquiring and accumulating artwork and collectibles can be as intriguing as the actual objects themselves. My pleasure in owning the Sears lithograph led to the subsequent purchase of a second

Daphnis and Chloe print from another, equally unexpected and uncharacteristic source.

Tucked away on Fifth Avenue, adjacent to the wholesale diamond district, was an innovative department store. Founded shortly after World War II, E. J. Korvette initiated a new concept in retail. Taking advantage of a loophole in existing statutes and defying prevailing fair-trade laws, the groundbreaking chain became the prototype for future discount venues such as Wal-Mart and Costco. Offering far greater reductions on comparable merchandise, Korvette consistently undercut the prices at more traditional department stores. Sued repeatedly by competitors such as Macy's, the young chain thrived on the attendant publicity, coverage that focused attention on its supposedly "illegally low" pricing.

Upon expanding the primarily suburban chain to Fifth Avenue, Korvette added home furnishings and decorative accessories to its traditional, more mundane offerings. That was how, quite by chance while shopping for a microwave oven, I stumbled across another delightfully tempting *Daphnis and Chloe* print offered at a remarkably reasonable price. I purchased the lithograph and have enjoyed living with it and its companion for more than fifty years. During that time, unforeseen and unpremeditated, the value of my modest investments has multiplied more than one hundredfold.

24

Unforeseen windfalls may be rare, but they do occur. Some years ago, browsing through a Christie's auction preview, I stumbled upon a set of thirty-six Japanese paintings that appeared to have been removed from an old scroll or album. The pictures, intricate and lovely, were included in the posthumous sale of someone's modest household estate. The estimate on the watercolors was minimal, so, as an interior designer and fine arts consultant who felt that the highly decorative group would be easy to divide and resell individually, I left a modest bid of fifteen hundred dollars. When the sale took place, mine was the only bid, and I acquired thirty-six lovely illustrations.

Subsequently, curious about the age and quality of my purchase, I consulted the curator of Japanese art at New York's Museum of Metropolitan Art. She presumed that the pictures dated from the 1920s and were likely the work of a student artist learning how to emulate an enviable earlier technique.

To my surprise, the curator telephoned shortly thereafter, inviting me to return to the Met to show my purchase to a highly respected expert visiting from one of Tokyo's principal museums. Upon arrival, I was ushered into a basement vault overflowing with treasured items. What a privilege to be able to view so many exquisite sequestered artifacts!

Seated on the floor beside the Japanese gentleman, I displayed my collection. With evident enthusiasm, he informed me that my paintings were, in fact, from the prized Kanō School, exquisite, and of considerable value. He offered me eight thousand dollars to purchase the set for his museum. The Metropolitan's curator suggested that I give them to the Metropolitan Museum as a charitable donation with a somewhat higher evaluation.

Since I had no way of knowing if the collection was complete, I did not hesitate to separate the set. Declining both offers, I eventually sold a few of the watercolors to clients for fifteen hundred dollars apiece, retaining a number of the paintings to hang in my own home, where they continue to delight me.

Recently, watching a telecast of Public Broadcasting's *Antiques Roadshow*, I witnessed a remarkably similar group of seventeenth-century paintings appraised "conservatively" at ten to twenty thousand dollars.

Some years after that rewarding purchase, while thrift shop browsing in south Florida, I noticed a small, signed, framed pencil drawing of a portly nude. The sketch, by Impressionist Jane Peterson, was priced at fifty dollars. I purchased it, then insured it for its actual value, some four thousand dollars. Lucky once again!

Fortuitous finds such as mine are not that uncommon, merely accidental and unpredictable. I believe that one should shop for collectibles with the heart, not the mind. If one covets an item and its price is acceptable, one should buy it simply for the pleasure of ownership. Whether a purchase will ultimately have greater or lesser value than its initial cost should be unimportant; the pleasure provided by its possession will dictate its true value.

25

Living in New York City I was privileged to encounter and converse with a diversity of recognizable people.

In the 1960s Jolie Gabor was my next-door neighbor and we became friends. I spent time with all three of her daughters and remember that Zsa Zsa, when asked how many husbands she had had, replied, nine in addition to her own. Zsa Zsa also bragged about having been a wonderful housekeeper; when she left a man, she invariably kept his house.

It was not unusual for me to encounter familiar figures while wandering about the city. Broadcaster Mike Wallace and author, editor, extravagant party giver George Plimpton lived nearby. I worked at *Harper's Bazaar* when fashion icons Carmel Snow (also a neighbor) and Diana Vreeland headed the magazine's editorial staff. Jacqueline Kennedy's sister Lee Radziwill and photographer Richard Avedon were friendly fellow employees. At *Harper's Bazaar,* I became the acquaintance, then client, of designer Oleg Cassini. Playing Bridge at the well-regarded Cavendish Club, I encountered fellow member, actor, and reputed card shark, Omar Sharif.

Active on a committee that oversaw the functions of a major charity, I conversed with co-administrator Joan Crawford. In the lavatory of a

Broadway theater, I traded critiques with fellow hand-washer, Mary Martin. Inadvertently sitting next to actor Mel Ferrer on a Madison Avenue bus gave rise to a casual, pleasant conversation. In the 1960s, when award-winning actor Robert Morse was performing in *How to Succeed in Business Without really Trying*, I became acquainted with him while baby-sitting for his infant daughter, Robin.

On a chilly February evening in 1957 Dick Isaacs, a public relations professional who was one of my regular escorts, invited me, along with two of his favorite clients, to dine at a popular Manhattan restaurant. Dick dealt primarily with the entertainment industry and our companions that evening were a charming young couple with whom we enjoyed an animated evening. A few weeks later, the woman, who had been visibly heavy with child, gave birth to a little girl. Over subsequent decades the couple, actors Christopher Plummer and Tammy Grimes, and their daughter Amanda all earned an amazing assortment of honors --- nominations and awards that encompassed multiple Oscars, Tonys, Emmys and Golden Globes.

In addition to First Lady, Ladybird Johnson, the waiting rooms of my doctors' offices enabled conversations with artist Andy Warhol, celebrity chef James Beard and author John Steinbeck (who graciously autographed one of his books and gave it to me).

In Manhattan unexpected sightings and encounters were anticipated. Seemingly routine, they constituted a diverting part of life.

26

Like so many facets of recent decades, air travel has changed dramatically. During the 1950s, when boarding international or lengthy flights, a lady's appropriate attire was respectfully formal and included a hat and gloves. Today, dress has become increasingly casual and far more comfortable, if less circumspect—occasionally bordering on the impermissible, if not the obscene.

Increasingly, today luggage is monitored, mishandled, and misdirected. While contemporary planes are much larger, faster, and more complex than when I began to fly, the comfort and duration of flights has not improved appreciably. From arriving at the departure airport with its preflight screening until exiting from the destination airport following luggage retrieval, a flight's overall elapsed time remains much the same as with older, far less innovative equipment. Pre-boarding seems interminable. Flights are frequently delayed. Until the 1970s, most security efforts were unnecessary and unobtrusive; one could pack for comfort and convenience rather than airport expediency. Today's seemingly endless pre-boarding lines and potentially intrusive examinations provide merely adequate insights and revelations.

In the old days, there was no charge for reasonable amounts of luggage. Substantial free meals, routinely served, have been replaced by paltry nibbles. As the flying population grows more obese, airplane seats have narrowed and legroom has diminished. When lowered, seatbacks increasingly encroach on resentful neighboring passengers. Omnipresent TVs have become a mixed blessing, as has the intrusive chatter and clatter of ubiquitous cell phones. Even the purchase of airline tickets is becoming more convoluted, acquiescing to the intricacies of the internet. Comfort has decreased; inconvenience has increased. Not merely my advancing age, but deflated comfort, inflated costs, increasingly complex routes, and potential terrorism are nurturing my waning enthusiasm for air travel.

Formerly a relatively enthusiastic flyer, I have become an increasingly reluctant one. Although most of my flights have been routine, I am the veteran of a number of memorable journeys.

During the 1930s, my first two flights were aboard modest, state-of-the-art, single-engine planes. Prior to takeoff, each passenger was given a parachute and reassuringly instructed how to don the device and employ it. As a result, my third flight was most unnerving; no parachutes were evident. When I confronted the stewardess, she informed me that, since passengers would be unlikely to jump out of a plane safely, parachutes, while continuing to be stowed beneath each seat, were no longer being demonstrated.

On two occasions, lightning struck the plane in which I was flying. During a violent thunderstorm over upstate New York, a powerful flash of electricity hit one wing as we struggled above mountainous terrain. Thankfully, despite marginal damage and no discernable place to make an emergency landing, the pilot maneuvered the DC-3 to the safety of a little-used Adirondack airport. Aboard a different DC-3, traveling between Rio de Janeiro and São Paulo, a powerful bolt of lightning crashed against the fuselage, causing significant damage. By chance, although we were not yet dating, I was seated alongside Joseph Jones, the man who eventually became my second husband. Fortuitously, neither of us was injured when the plane lurched forward and plummeted. Prophetically, our mutual friend, Nelson Rockefeller, had cautioned me to avoid any flight if Joe Jones was on board: "When Joe flies, something unwarranted always seems to happen." (Fortunately for me, countless subsequent flights with Joe proved uneventful.)

On two separate occasions, I found myself in full, if relatively brief, control of a commercial airliner. As the lone passenger on a small Brazilian plane returning from Porto Alegre to São Paulo, the flirtatious pilot invited me to sit in the unoccupied co-pilot seat and amused himself by teaching me how to maneuver the aircraft. Years later, on a crowded, partially disabled Constellation traveling over the Amazonian wilderness, I was recruited to operate the plane. When the pilot (who had befriended me before the flight) became ill, and all remaining crewmembers were otherwise engaged, I was surreptitiously drafted to take charge of the conveyance. Because the automatic pilot was disabled and the compass malfunctioning, I had to exercise full control of the aircraft for several hours, keeping it steady, at an appropriate altitude, and on course. Reluctantly, if nervously, I complied with my instructions. Having become cognizant of what unorthodox procedures might occur during a presumably routine flight, I never again felt totally at ease in the air.

On a flight to Chicago, the jumbo jet on which I was traveling developed significant mechanical problems. After circling the field to discharge excess fuel, the plane bounced precariously onto a snow-slippery airstrip judiciously remote from the terminal and active runways. Shaken and obliged to exit via an emergency slide, I suffered what seemed a minor injury. Referred to a physician, who turned out to be an inept chiropractor, my minor spinal grievance acerbated, resulting in paralysis from the waist down. Transported back to New York, a lengthy hospital stay ensued during which I had to relearn how to walk.

At the behest of my American orthopedist, rehabilitation eventually took me to a spa in Romania, where, while the last traces of my paralysis were cured, I developed a severe case of pneumonia. Since the quality of local English-speaking medical care was dubious, I sought succor at the American embassy in Bucharest where staff suggested I be moved to either London or Paris. President and Mrs. Nixon, visiting Europe on a goodwill tour, happened to be in town, scheduled to fly to Great Britain that evening. Due to complicated logistics and incredible coincidences—I already enjoyed top security clearance and was casually acquainted with both the president and the first lady—it was suggested that I be medevacked to a British hospital aboard Air Force One. Ill as I was, I declined the offer in favor of returning to Paris (where I had numerous friends) for my remedial treatment and recuperation.

More recently, while intending to explore remote Mayan ruins in Guatemala's hinterlands, I fell while attempting to climb into a dilapidated, archaic aircraft. As I tried to mount, the plane's rickety metal stairs gave way, and I was catapulted onto an uneven, dangerously rock-littered landing strip. Severely bruised and bleeding, I became entangled in the airplane's broken ladder. Remote from civilization, I was obliged to continue cautiously on a tenuous, physically painful journey during which I was caringly—though crudely—patched and ministered to by kind concerned locals.

27

Nothing has advanced more dramatically during my lifetime than the practice of medicine. Ailments have changed, new ones have arisen, therapies have kept evolving. Since the 1930s, life expectancy in the United States has risen from 60 years to more than 78 years.

When I was very young, one of my mother's closest friends was Stella Schwartz, who lived in an apartment building directly across the street from us. Mother visited Stella regularly, and occasionally, on Nanny's afternoons off, Mommy would walk me across Park Avenue for a visit. We always found frail Aunt Stella propped against a pile of pillows in her immaculate, wrinkle-free, snow-white bed. She was cheerful and fun to be with, but she was whisper-voiced, and I was not permitted to kiss or even touch her. She had tuberculosis. In the 1930s and early 1940s--before streptomycin and other yet to be developed antibiotics--tuberculosis was not uncommon and was considered potentially, if not eventually, deadly. TB was isolating. Affluent victims often chose to recuperate in Switzerland. Others went to dedicated sanatoriums scattered about the United States in cool, dry, relatively isolated locations. One of those facilities was located not far from our summer retreat in the Adirondack Mountains, and, warily, when driving through the area, my family would give it a wide-birth. What was unusual about Stella's approach to her illness was that, despite being well off financially, she chose to remain in New York City, cared for in her lifelong residence. By the time that I was old enough to enter grade school, consumption had taken her life.

During my youth, poliomyelitis was another dreaded ailment. A worldwide disease, not necessarily fatal, it often left victims with extensive residual damage. My eighteen-year-old cousin Louise, who barely survived a virulent attack, was left frail and subject to assorted complications for the remainder of her life. In the early 1950s, while visiting Brazil, I fell sufficiently ill to summon a physician to evaluate and treat me. Although unconfirmed since I recovered quickly, I was thought to be suffering from polio. If true, mine was a remarkably mild case and left no residual aftereffects. When the Salk vaccine became available, I became one of its early recipients.

I have survived--both figuratively and literally--a number of my physicians. Contrary to what has become increasingly commonplace, I would neither trust nor patronize a physician (or lawyer or financial adviser) who advertises for clients. Reliable recommendations, sincere word-of-mouth referrals are and always have been my criteria.

While of utmost importance, it is not always easy to be satisfied with one's medical practitioners. For many years, while extremely proficient and charming, my principal doctor was so excessively compassionate, so empathetic, that I had trouble communicating with him, fearful of distressing the man. As a result of my reticence some significant problems were almost overlooked.

While somewhat reluctant to visit doctors, I have always liked going to the dentist. As a preschooler, I had poor teeth and a wonderful dentist. If one of my baby teeth was ready to be ejected, he offered salt-water taffy as an extractor. When a filling was necessary, Dr. Posen would hand me a small mirror, instructing me to hold it in a tricky, very specific position so that I could watch and assist the entire procedure. Although difficult, it was important for me to hold the mirror correctly--I was substituting for the doctor's reliable but otherwise occupied, starchily uniformed nurse. What small girl didn't want to wear a nurse's uniform? I wanted to earn the crisp, white signature cap. Entranced, I was eager to demonstrate that I was sufficiently mature, capable, and sophisticated for the job! Absorbed, I had no awareness of discomfort, never noticing pain if, indeed, there was any. Well indoctrinated, I have never felt tense or apprehensive in a dental chair. It is where I relax, even dozing off during protracted, non-anesthetized procedures.

In my twenties, I went to a New York dental surgeon to have an impacted wisdom tooth removed. The doctor insisted upon placing a mask over my face and administering an inhalable sedative. When the procedure was complete, I regained consciousness, speaking only Portuguese. It took five to ten minutes--during which time the dentist and I were utterly perplexed--before I could remember, readjust, and communicate in my native English.

Years earlier in Brazil, being prepared to minimize the discomfort of another procedure, I found myself sitting on a cushion on the floor of my doctor's office in São Paulo where, at the doctor's insistence, he and I inhaled opium from a large hookah. The intent was to calm and anesthetize me before employing an intimidating wire instrument to drain my sinuses. The vapors had their desired effect; I enjoyed the smoke, and neither felt nor recalled anything negative about the procedure.

During the 1960s, to correct her clouding eyesight, my aging mother underwent cataract surgery. For a number of days following each of two widely separated procedures, she was confined to a hospital bed with cumbersome sandbags placed on her pillow to ensure her head remained immobilized. Thanks to the introduction of lasers and other medical advances, when I had my cataracts removed some fifty years later, the two procedures were performed merely weeks apart. Immediately following early morning surgeries, accompanied by a friend who drove, I enjoyed relaxed lunches at a neighborhood restaurant.

Medications, especially sedatives, can be unpredictable, inducing unanticipated consequences. Take Halcion and Ambien, for example. Suffering from insomnia, my husband was prescribed one or another of the sedatives, and, on at least two occasions, sleepwalking followed by amnesia ensued. In both instances, my extremely conservative, proper spouse managed to embarrass himself.

When a childhood friend of mine, a voluptuous blond, was residing in the guestroom at the far side of our home, Joe, sedated and wandering about in the still of night, entered her room and slipped affectionately into bed beside her. Awakened by the ensuing commotion, I rationalized that, because at one time, he and I had used that room as our master bedroom, Joe must have fancied that he was returning to me.

A second incident was more disconcerting. Hospitalized for a heart-related problem, a restless Joe was given Ambien to induce slumber. Sound asleep, he discarded his hospital attire and proceeded to stroll, stark naked, around much of the institution before being apprehended, awakened, bundled in blankets, and returned to his bed.

28

As one ages, out of caution if not necessity, one becomes more circumspect regarding health and overall wellbeing. This is especially true when visiting far-flung, often exotic destinations. While traveling abroad during our senior years, my husband and I each endured our share of physical emergencies--usually with fortunate, fortuitous results.

Joe and I both suffered heart attacks while vacationing in Europe. Although some years apart, each of the two episodes occurred in Germany. In typically female fashion, I had no idea I had suffered an attack until it was diagnosed a few months later during a routine doctor's visit. Evidently, the problem occurred while I was towing cumbersome luggage and racing between connecting flights in the Stuttgart airport. At the time, I was aware that my arm hurt, I was short of breath, and had mild chest discomfort, but I attributed those symptoms to stress and excessive exertion.

A few years later, I underwent emergency heart bypass surgery. In Palm Beach at the time, I was rushed into treatment with no choice as to hospital or surgeon. As usual, I was extremely fortunate; I underwent a brand-new procedure, arthroscopic minimal bypass surgery. The only scar, hidden under my breast, was less than half an inch in length and has since disappeared completely. Without any postoperative medication, other than a single Tylenol, I never felt pain during recuperation, only a slight itching as my skin healed. I was up and around almost immediately. At the time, the technique was so revolutionary that I was asked to be interviewed, along with my physician, by Tom Brokaw on NBC television's national Nightly News. I declined, and the doctor appeared with another patient.

Joe's attack was far more serious. It occurred shortly after we checked into the Brenners Park Hotel in Baden-Baden. My husband was so tall that the hotel's minuscule elevators could not accommodate his stretcher, and paramedics were forced to evacuate him via the elaborate grand staircase. Rushed by ambulance to a local hospital, Joe remained in precarious condition for about a week. Not only did he receive the best of care from an always cheerful and affectionate medical staff, but the nurses and doctors pampered and fussed over me as well. So did the hotel. The Brenners Park staff kept checking to make sure I was all right, physically, and emotionally. They would not even allow me to pay for my twice-daily limousine commutes to the distant hospital. Weeks later, when Joe was cleared to fly home to the United States, I exchanged our Air France business class passage for what I presumed would be a more comfortable and less challenging experience in first class. As it turned out, we were the sole passengers assigned to the jet's upper deck. It was like having our own private aircraft. Imagine the transatlantic luxury of a staff of one's own, seats that could be combined into beds, food at one's whim, and, above all, the luxury of a completely private, meticulously maintained lavatory.

Typical of my frequent inadvertent encounters with notable people, on two separate occasions, a show-business celebrity saved me from probable injury and possible death. Years ago, in the nick of time, movie hero Van Johnson pulled me out of the path of a speeding automobile that had ignored a red light and was aimed directly at me as I crossed Manhattan's

Lexington Avenue. A few decades later, while lunching aboard ship during an Atlantic crossing, I began to choke. Perceiving that I could neither breathe adequately nor help myself, a gentleman seated at an adjacent table leaped up and successfully administered the Heimlich maneuver. My rescuer was stage and television star, Jerry Orbach.

In addition to modern medical advances, time-honored traditional treatments continue to provide succor. Throughout the last decade of his life, Joe's damaged knees caused him constant pain, presumably the result of an old automobile accident compounding youthful football injuries. He needed knee replacements, but cardiac irregularities proscribed all optional surgery. One particularly painful day, while cruising the South Pacific, the captain of our ship, noticing Joe's extreme discomfort, handed him a small bottle containing dark green, eucalyptus-scented oil, and directed my husband to rub a few drops onto the painful areas. Skeptically, Joe did as instructed. To his amazement, he found himself pain-free within minutes. For the remainder of his life, Chinese Green Oil became his routine salvation.

Plagued by chronic sciatica and inspired by Joe's results, I decided to experiment with the analgesic myself. Success! Subsequently, I discovered that a single drop of the soothing blend of menthol, camphor, and eucalyptus, when placed between my eyebrows, prevented or alleviated migraine headaches, while a few droplets rubbed around my bellybutton relieved the queasiness of seasickness.

Impossible? Perhaps, but even if relief is purely in the mind, the green oil works for me and for many others to whom I have given it. I always keep a bottle close at hand.

29

During my twenties and thirties, even during my married but childless forties, most of my close friends and companions were male. Most of my female acquaintances were married and thoroughly absorbed in childcare and domesticity, while the men were predictably more dynamic and world-oriented, more compatible, more stimulating.

Single for thirty-nine years, in addition to casual male friends, I dated a surprisingly diverse assortment of gentlemen. There were Jews, Gentiles, and a Muslim; North Americans, South Americans, Europeans, and an aristocrat from Kenya; an inventor; a composer; a Nobel Prize nominee; a Washington D.C. powerbroker; two foreign statesmen; minor relatives of European royalty; a famous movie star; more than one former spy, and descendants of three famous individuals.

As a teenager in Brazil, I dated Roberto Eduardo Lee, direct descendent of General Robert E. Lee. Although the Confederate general had advised southerners against fleeing the United States at the end of the Civil War, Roberto's ancestors were among the ten thousand or more disheartened United States landowners who migrated to South America in 1865. At the time, encouraged by Brazil's Emperor Dom Pedro II, the two to three-week voyage to Brazil cost between twenty and thirty dollars. While many of those who fled ultimately returned north, some ninety-four families remained in Brazil, prospered, and, known as the *Confederados* (Confederates), became thoroughly assimilated citizens of Brazil. My friendship with Roberto evolved because our fathers enjoyed a social as well as a business relationship. Some three decades after our teenage dates, no longer in touch with one another, I learned that Roberto--prosperous, socially prominent, and a philander-er--had been slain by a companion's jealous husband.

At eighteen, romanced by Arturo Toscanini's grandson Walfredo, I was privileged to become acquainted with the feisty maestro (who surreptitiously pinched my buttocks suggestively while we were pressed together in a tiny European elevator). During subsequent summers, vacationing in Tuscany, I dined and danced with a hereditary Italian Prince and, in Portugal, dated a member of that former royal family.

During early visits to London my father's friend the Fifth Lord Grey, descendant of the former Prime minister after whom the tea had been named, introduced me to a young man named Geffen. At the time, my escort was also socializing with Princess Margaret Rose and the high-profile Margret Set. Geffen's whispered, intimate, and often unflattering confidences about the princess, her disposition, and her emotional attachments were always interesting and occasionally shocking. Although I was not aware of it at the time, a recent article in the *New York Times* revealed that Geffen's ancestors had somehow included the hapless Queen Anne Boleyn.

While in my twenties, I spent time with a number of men who had been spies during the Second World War. One, a former U2 pilot, had shared a plane and a mission with Francis Gary Powers. Prominent German TV newsman, author, and statesman, Klaus Mehnert, an Allies-decorated double agent, was a frequent companion. Still another of my escorts had been a participant in Operation Mincemeat, the climactic and decisive undercover

World War II maneuver recounted in the 1956 film *The Man Who Never Was.* Among the more creative and frequent of my companions were Lawrence Goldmuntz (a designer of the Dew Line and inventor of the Laser), scientific Nobel Prize contender Walter Freygang, and Luiz Bonfá, composer of music for the Brazilian movie *Orfeo Negro* (*Black Orpheus*). During the late 1950s, I dined, danced, swam, attended movies, and played challenging trivia games with an extremely compatible Roy Fitzgerald, better known to the world as movie idol Rock Hudson.

Although eager to find true love, to settle down and raise children, with so many interesting gentlemen in my life, I was far from lonely, never bored, and cautiously reluctant to commit myself to an exclusive, permanent relationship. When I finally did commit, I chose unwisely but--a decade and a divorce later--found fulfillment in an idyllic second marriage.

30

My first marriage was to Edward Kean, creator, writer, composer, and lyricist of the children's television classic *Howdy Doody*. At the time we met, Ed, no longer involved in show business, was working as a Wall Street stockbroker. Divorced, he had two young children. It was his eleven-year-old daughter, Patricia, who initially suggested that her father and I marry. Nine years later, following the breakup of our marriage, I continued to maintain contact with both children and, eventually, with their offspring.

My initial encounter with Joseph Jones, who became my second husband, took place aboard the steamship *Brazil* when we were assigned to dine together at the Chief Engineer's table. Joe was traveling with his wife and two young daughters. We became casual friends and, after returning to our then current domiciles in São Paulo, the Joneses and I continued to socialize.

Unexpectedly, Joe's wife, a staunch Roman Catholic unwilling to initiate divorce, alienated me by seeking my help in finding a woman for whom her no longer desired husband would abandon her. Appalled, I resolved to terminate all encounters with the Jones family.

Despite attempted avoidance, due to inadvertent simultaneous stays in the same Rio de Janeiro hotel, accompanied by over-lapping social engagements initiated by mutual Carioca friends, Joe and I continued to run into one another. Hesitantly, cautiously, somewhat uneasily, we began to reconnect.

Although neither of us acknowledged our feelings--even to ourselves--Joe and I had been attracted to one another from the moment we first met. As we spent renewed time together, our initially sublimated emotions evolved into a passionate on-again-off-again love affair. Eventually, after many emotionally and socially complex years, Joe obtained a divorce and, in 1985, twenty-six years after our first encounter, we sanctified our enduring friendship, our affection, and devotion, with matrimony.

Our marriage affected me in unexpected ways. Unlike my assertive mother, I had never been competitive, had never felt comfortable challenging anyone other than myself. Although proficient at tennis, Ping-Pong, and Bridge, I always recoiled at the prospect of defeating an opponent. Ambitious and a perfectionist, I wanted to be victorious, but not at the expense of defeating a rival. Shy and self-conscious, I knew how to lose graciously but was unsure how to win diplomatically. Although I always made a sincere effort to defeat my adversaries, I was loath to raise my visibility by vanquishing a rival. I deliberately lost most contests during the final moments. Not wishing to let partners down, I genuinely attempted to win only when playing Bridge or competing at doubles in tennis.

In mid-life, as Joe's consort and constant companion, I began to pursue victory. With a competitive spouse, I enjoyed the challenge and frequent frustration of attempting to best (usually unsuccessfully) my capable and competitive husband. Joe rarely, if ever, lost at anything. Highly skilled and intelligent, whether at work or play, Joe, always gracious, seldom needed to accept defeat. Even when competing with very young grandchildren (whom he gently but sternly felt should learn how to handle the reality of losing at an early age), he played to win. Attempting to out-maneuver Joe, I became more adept, incisive, and resourceful.

Joe taught me to be less reclusive, less reticent, calmer, more coura-geous, and more self-assured. I taught him to be less protective of his emo-tions, to be unafraid of feeling and revealing previously secreted sensitivities. Prior to our friendship, Joe had never felt safe allowing himself to care deeply or to demonstrate his innermost emotions. Evidently, neither his parents nor his first wife had displayed or satisfactorily communicated affection. Long before we married, as friends, then lovers, he and I had begun to influence and transform one another. When together, we encouraged, exposed, and enhanced each other's otherwise guarded feelings.

Joe and I exemplified the maxim "opposites attract." While our tastes and mores were alike, our temperaments and dispositions, our approaches to life, were truly Yin and Yang: contrasting, yet complementary and supportive. We consistently brought out the best in one another.

31

My marriage to Edward Kean ended abruptly, with no warning. I was sleeping late one mid-winter morning when Ed awakened me by placing an unexpected present next to me on the bed. The gratuitous gift was a darling Yorkshire puppy. My husband's motivation for the gift was as unanticipated as the gift itself. During the night, he had packed his belongings and was leaving me for another woman. Since we had executed a pre-nuptial agreement, the imminent divorce would be swift and nonconfrontational. The dog was intended to assuage Ed's guilt, to mitigate the depression he assumed would result from his departure. It was my husband's egotistical attempt to replace his presumably irreplaceable self. He thought the puppy would supply me with the love, warmth, affection, and companionship he was no longer in a position to provide.

Stunned, despite years of gradually increasing estrangement, I was unexpectedly relieved by the unforeseen situation and wished Ed well in the revival of his romance with a former girlfriend. Although I loved dogs, anticipating incipient freedom, I declined the adorable puppy, unwilling to incur the restrictions and responsibilities that its adoption would entail.

That snow darkened Sunday continued to be one of the strangest days of my life. Shortly after noon my telephone rang. It was Klaus Mehnert, the prominent German journalist and statesman, calling from Aachen. He and I had been out of touch for ten years.

"I've been thinking about you," he volunteered. "I sense that you may need me to comfort you, to boost your ego, to let you know how desirable and special you are, so I've booked a flight to New York to spend time with you. To camouflage the real reason for my trip, I've arranged a visit with President Carter at the White House. See you in a couple of days."

Scarcely an hour later, I received an even more amazing call, this time from Joseph Jones, my former lover who was living in Tokyo. He and I had been out of contact for more than a decade.

"Now that you're free to see me, I'm anxious to be with you. Please say you'll dine with me if I come to the States!"

At that juncture, not even my mother, who lived only a few blocks from me, suspected that my marriage was foundering, much less that it was at an end. Even I had been surprised. How on earth did two physically distant, totally incommunicado but formerly intimate friends know the precise moment at which my marriage collapsed? Extrasensory perception seemed the only explanation.

During the days and weeks that followed, Klaus and I renewed our quiescent friendship. Carefully, cautiously, then ardently, Joe and I rekindled our intermittent attachment. In due time, following mutual divorces, we married and lived devotedly ever after.

32

I have enjoyed an assortment of memorable meals, some recalled because of the food, others for their location or ambiance.

Among the countless restaurants scattered throughout Paris, there were two that I remember for the high quality and significant limitations of their offerings. One of them, set high on a twisting alleyway in Montmartre, occupied a narrow open-windowed space above a small ground floor boutique. Once inside, one could order fine wines, to complement which the proprietress would select suitable cheeses, or one could request an assortment of exceptionally fine, often rare cheeses for which the hostess would dictate appropriate wines. Sated, one exited by way of the downstairs shop that sold only the finest liquors and cheeses. The second highly specialized restaurant, dark and cozy even at lunchtime, was situated on the Right Bank, near the Louvre. It was called Le Soufflé, and, indeed, soufflés were the only offering. There would be some sort of miniature appetizer soufflé, followed by a pretentiously puffed main course and an intriguingly plump and airy dessert.

My two most memorable oriental meals were served oceans apart, one in Japan and the other in Great Britain. In Tokyo, my first *kaiseki* meal was stunning, not only visually, but financially; in the early 1990s, the luncheon for two that cost upwards of $400 is memorable primarily for its "foreign-ness." It consisted of fourteen traditional courses, many of which incorpo-rated provisions and preparations previously unfamiliar to me. Despite my husband's forewarning, being served food that was still alive was a shock. There were bowls filled with what appeared to be rice until one realized that the erstwhile kernels were moving and had tiny dark eyes; they were live baby eels. Additionally, there was a generous platter of colorful sashimi surrounding the *piece-de-resistance*, a large lobster. Its spine cracked open, the lobster was still alive and eagerly stretching its claws in an attempt to devour pieces of the surrounding salmon, squid, and tuna. Appalled, I chose to leave the table while my husband, who, having lived in Japan, was accustomed to--and not intimidated by--Japanese cuisine, ate the unquestionably fresh, still hungry crustacean.

In celebration of the fortieth anniversary of our high school grad-uation, my former Horace Mann-Lincoln classmates decided to gather in Manhattan for a celebratory class reunion. Among the few alumni resid-ing overseas, all but one accepted the invitation. Unfortunately, Chaozhu responded that his duties as the Chinese ambassador to the Court of St. James prevented him from leaving England. Instead, he invited us to visit him in London, where he would entertain us and host a second reunion. Some thirty of us, with spouses, accepted. Once abroad, thanks to Chaozhu, we were handsomely entertained by numerous members of the British aris-tocracy, including the Duke of Bedford, who invited us to a relaxed lunch in his home, Woburn Abbey, followed by a visit to the zoo on his palatial country estate.

The reunion dinner itself was an unforgettable meal. Elegantly served at the Chinese Embassy, the banquet--a visually spectacular, aromatically intriguing, delicious, and munificent array of often unfamiliar dishes--was, we were informed, identical to one served to Queen Elizabeth II during a state visit to the embassy.

During a different visit to London, my husband and I enjoyed another noteworthy repast, an elegant white tie dinner-dance at Blenheim Palace, the Churchill family's grand country estate. Hosted by the property's owner, the Duke of Marlborough, together with the royal Duke of Kent, each guest's arrival, as well as dinner itself, was formally announced in thunderous voice by an aging sergeant-at-arms in full scarlet and gold, medal heavy, regalia. Because the June night was unseasonably cool and the sprawling mansion somewhat drafty, its sequence of splendid chambers, warmed by flickering fires, seemed cozy and welcoming despite the attendant pomp and ceremony. The meal, served in a stately dining hall replete with numerous peers of the realm and familiar faces from stage, screen, and government, was delightfully friendly and relaxed. The food was excellent but not nearly as exceptional as our erstwhile dinner at the Chinese embassy.

Years earlier, while touring Portugal on a lazy summer day, a girlfriend and I stopped for lunch in a sleepy fishing village where small boats and rugged surfers shared the waves and the sprawling beach. Hungry, we found a tiny restaurant and seated ourselves at a rickety table on a porch overlooking the sea. Aware that the area was known for its sardines, we ordered the local specialty. The hole-in-the-wall's proprietor smiled and, scurrying across the sand, waded into the surf to bargain--arms waving, fingers flashing--with one of the arriving fishermen. When satisfied, our host returned, his mesh sack dripping with flapping fish. Disappearing into the kitchen, he reemerged moments later with mouthwatering platters of steaming, unquestionably fresh sardines.

Another of my more memorable meals--memorable not only for its discriminating flavors but for its elegance of execution--was served in a most unlikely place, aboard an airplane. During a charter flight over Antarctica, seated comfortably in a window seat and gazing down at impressive ice formations interrupted by unexpectedly generous expanses of dark earth and waddling penguins, I was plied with seemingly endless French champagne, Iranian caviar, Argentinian steak, and a huge, generous-clawed Brazilian lobster. Each course was accompanied by an exquisite array of side dishes and embellishments. Each tray was decorated with a fragrant summer rose.

There were other unforgettable meals, such as a tented dinner amid seemingly endless, wind-sculpted sand dunes in the Namibian desert; a Roman luncheon in the graceful ruins of a three-thousand-year-old temple dedicated to the Vestal Virgins; a merely mediocre meal in a shack propped against the Great Wall of China; and dinner in glamorous venues like Windows on the World atop New York's long since demolished World Trade Center.

The most archaic dinner I can recall was served in the heart of France. Joe and I were spending the night in an aging Chateau situated on a sprawling farm in the heart of Burgundy. The medieval dwelling that occasionally functioned as a makeshift bed-and-breakfast had never been modernized. Generous supplies of firewood and partially melted candles compensated for the absence of both gas and electricity. All cooking was done over burning wood, primarily in the vast feudal fireplace that dominated the soaring main hall.

Our host was a rather stuffy, retired minor French official who, years before, had been stationed in the Far East. While in Vietnam, he met and married a much younger woman from a prosperous, local, servant-enabled family. His bride had not the slightest notion of how to boil water, much less how to prepare a proper meal. Gastronomically demanding, and fancying himself a connoisseur, Monsieur gave his wife a copy of the classic French cookbook *Larousse Gastrominic,* ordering her to teach herself to cook. Learn she did. By the time we were guests in their antiquated French estate, Madame had become such a fine, internationally acclaimed chef that a number of her specialties (particularly her *paté de fois gras*) were being successfully exported for sale worldwide.

On the night of our visit, seated around a time-defaced refractory table, we watched as our hostess prepared dinner in the vast, smoke-darkened fireplace. The superb six-course meal consisted entirely of locally raised and harvested seafood, livestock, and produce. While we sipped wine and exchanged mundane anecdotes in colloquial French, Madame grilled the fish, seared the meats, and steamed the vegetables over softly crackling flames.

Before dinner, admiring the sunset, we had enjoyed cocktails on a summer warmed terrace, watching as fresh strawberries from the garden and rich cream from a resident cow were blended inside an old-fashioned, hand-cranked, wooden ice-cream churn. Using ice that had been salvaged from a winter lake and stored, protected by sawdust, in a small shed, the mixture was converted into our extremely rich and succulent dessert. After dinner, there were Cuban cigars accompanied by brandies whose bottles, to maintain the liqueur at a suitable temperature, had been stored in the cool earth beneath detachable parlor floorboards.

33

As Joe and I aged, dealing with progressively strenuous cooking and cleaning, home maintenance, and nighttime driving became increasingly burdensome. Following decades of enjoyable world travel, our enthusiasm and eagerness for touring began to wane. Impulsively, reacting to the aftermath of an especially virulent hurricane that had threatened (but not seriously damaged) our beachfront condominium, we sold our home and moved to Devonshire, a well-reputed local retirement community.

Life in an indulgent senior life care facility like the one into which Joe and I moved resembled life aboard a luxurious ocean liner. Daily needs and desired diversions were conscientiously catered to. With household responsibilities and physical necessities satisfied, stress was minimized. In a world dominated by ever-increasing physical and philosophical challenges, both privacy and agreeable social interaction remained accessible. The atmosphere was friendly and relaxed, supportive, but never invasive. We were surrounded by neighbors, survivors like ourselves, who were fashioning new friendships with compatible fellow elders, people with similar lifestyles but with intriguingly dissimilar backgrounds and histories.

Most of our neighbors were successful, well-established, often self-made retirees, indulged wives and widows, or providentially raised progeny like me. Having experienced widely divergent lifestyles, we had sundry memories and viewpoints to share. We exemplified a complex, often intriguing generation. The *mise en scène* of our lives--worldwide conflict offset by significant technical and artistic achievement combined with debatable moral modification--had molded us all.

Because memories can be both faulty and selective, our "good old days" may not have been quite as auspicious as we recollected. It is important that we not permit reminiscences to minimize and denigrate the present. Maturing individuals need to adapt to age-adjusting minds and bodies, to spousal demises. Residents need to remain socially active and involved, neither confusing nor substituting isolation for privacy. Neighbors who share the modifications and tribulations of advancing age provide companionship, comfort, and consolation to one another. Having become a widow, I continue to find Devonshire friendly and hospitable.

Although single men are welcome to socialize and dine with committed couples, the inclusion of single women is somewhat more problematic. Secure wives welcome the companionship of single ladies, relieved that their husband's old, repetitious, and by now overly familiar jokes and reminiscences can be genuinely appreciated by someone new. Less secure wives shudder at the prospect of socializing with potentially aggressive, man-hungry competitors. Single men often favor the companionship of other gentlemen.

On occasion, the qualms of wary wives are justified. Some reluctantly single women are indeed on the prowl. The moment a new man moves in, or an aging female partner dies or succumbs to dementia, the needy and sometimes lustful women implement all manner of hopefully captivating behavior. A number of ensuing romances have resulted. A few of the pairings have developed into seemingly happy marriages, others into equally contented coupling.

In one instance, a recently widowed neighbor, the survivor of a long and unsatisfying marriage that, for one reason or another, she had declined to terminate, eagerly paired herself with a newly arrived widower. Their relationship quickly developed into an ostentatious, giggling, handholding, waist-encircling affair with the ecstatic lady boasting that never in her entire life had she been so happy:

"I'm in heaven! He not only sends me flowers; he lends me his heating pad!"

As one ages, needs and behaviors change. Similar to affairs of the very young, affection among the elderly may be pretentious. There are genuinely devoted, discretely caring couples--many of them longtime second pairings following the deaths of former spouses. They hold hands and share affectionate appellations and glances in public while other, deliberately ostentatious couples blatantly engage in conspicuous sexual innuendo. Far from being embarrassed by their brazen displays, these paramours, seemingly well into second childhoods, behave like immature teenagers seeking to recapture and flaunt youthful, long obsolete, macho or femme fatale reputations.

Anticipating being snubbed by exclusionary couples, some single women defensively, if often needlessly, band together, retreating into feminine cliques. With advancing age, ladies of my generation, raised with an emphasis on propriety, decorum, and at least a façade of (possibly pseudo) innocence, begin to enjoy more liberated socializing. Gossip and innuendo abound. Less disciplined conversations become far more risqué, wicked, and indiscreet. Vocabulary may relax, shock, and incorporate the formerly salacious.

Admired, if simultaneously pitied and looked down upon, are residents who attach themselves firmly and possessively to failing, physically decrepit, virtually incompetent, non-spousal partners. Although these caregivers receive little obvious benefit from their ministrations, they appear obsessive in the constant companionship and prodigious attention they lavish upon grateful recipients. Neighbors often presume these kind custodians, particularly the women, are fortune hunters. I believe that most are pitifully lonely and insecure. Desperate to find a purpose in life, they are self-deprecating and nurture a profound need to be needed, to be validated, to feel equal if not superior to and more fortunate than someone--anyone--else.

Inevitably, during the years I have resided in Devonshire, changes and modifications have ensued. Long-time residents have aged. Initially forbidden, walkers and wheelchairs have become commonplace, though intrusive, encumbering passageways and public areas. While I consider the clutter physically inconvenient, unlike neighbors who find the sight of proliferating supportive equipment depressing, I view the appliances cheerfully, evidence that my aging fellow residents are still active and, although cautious, are participating in life.

Recently, I overheard a fellow tenant attempting to persuade a physically impaired potential occupant to relocate and move to Devonshire. Enumerating various advantages, the resident assured the applicant that both physical and emotional assistance were available:

"A lot of people here have aides."

Visibly upset, the visitor cried out, "AIDs? How dreadful! Thank you for the warning! I wouldn't dream of moving in!"

Seemingly, Devonshire's idealized, somewhat artificial environment adds years--worthwhile years--to already-lengthy lives. A ninety-five-year-old neighbor recently informed me that he feels amiss since giving up golf one year ago and tennis when he was "only ninety-three." On the day following his one-hundredth birthday, another neighbor played three holes of golf. At least four couples have been married for more than seventy years, and, at weekend ballroom dances, one of those couples--wed for seventy-seven years--still pirouettes gracefully and energetically to an animated lindy hop.

A number of sprightly neighbors have passed the century mark. On Saturday nights, a lithe one-hundred-year-old lady twirls gracefully to multiple rhythms partnered by one of the visiting dance hosts. Another charmingly youthful centenarian is always meticulously groomed and stylishly dressed. At one-hundred-and-two, she is careful to ensure that her eye shadow invariably matches the color of her outfit. Each day, following exercise in the gymnasium, an unwrinkled one-hundred-and-one year-old gentleman goes swimming. At one-hundred-and-six, another gentleman gives me more astute, updated financial advice than either my banker or my stockbroker. Blessed with reasonably good fortune, good surroundings, and guarded good health, I perceive that the advent of advancing age is not inevitably daunting.

34

When I moved into Devonshire, I acquired a necklace anchored by a safety pendant. Except when climbing a ladder or undertaking some other risky or foolish activity, I left the piece unworn and abandoned in a bureau drawer. After all, my apartment was equipped with a scattering of emergency call buttons, and I was neither unsteady nor given to dizziness. In my mid-eighties, I was still young and healthy. However, recently and reluctantly--pressured by neighbors who kept reminding me that, since falls are not uncommon in the elderly, we should all be as cautious as possible--I have been persuaded to hang the alarm around my neck whenever I am alone in my apartment.

Initially, this accommodation had a profound emotional effect on me. Rather than making me feel safe, the pendant became a constant reminder of how vulnerable I am. Suddenly, I viewed myself as a truly old lady and an incipiently feeble one. No longer could I enjoy my erstwhile youthful, if delusive, self-assessment.

Wearing the pendant made me feel timeworn and doddering. It made me feel I was failing and that, inevitably, I would accidentally injure myself, a misadventure that was only a matter of *when* not *if*. Wearing the tiny disc prompted me to review my will and my end of life directives; to update, clarify and de-clutter my files; to rid my surroundings of useless, albeit sentimental, keepsakes; to define and discard seldom donned clothing. The limited and limiting remainder of my life became of persistent, if subliminal, awareness. I was not in the least frightened nor saddened, but rather more inhibited and constrained. I began to reflect upon my rich and active past more contentedly than I contemplated an ambitious future. Potential projects necessitating significant effort tended to seem excessive, even futile. I finally recognized that I am old.

This rather negative response endured for a time, but gradually my attitude changed. I came to recognize that "inside every older person is a younger person wondering what the hell happened!" The pendant, now welcome, hangs reassuringly around my neck whenever I am alone. It emboldens me; it relaxes me; it makes me feel safe. I have become more ambitious. Sensing that I can be more adventurous because of the pendant's protection, I assert myself more. Increasingly, far from inhibiting and depressing me, the pendant is enabling and enriching my life.

35

At Devonshire privacy and prudence can be inconsistent. In the residents' crowded breakfast venue with its aroma of burnt toast and freshly brewed coffee gossip is rampant. Whether haunting or humorous, fearful or cheerful, revealing exchanges expose not merely the targets but the tattlers.

This became particularly notable during heated controversies that arose during the Trump presidency. It was impossible for those who feared and detested the President's seemingly demented and dishonest performance to comprehend the continuing loyalty of presumably intelligent, well-informed, well-schooled contemporaries.

Controversial politics aside, amid the clatter of chinaware and the chatter of colleagues, anecdotes abound. Lives and lifestyles, exploits and adventures, historic events, are consistently if randomly --- and far too often erroneously --- recounted. While falsified tales of the past are usually a matter of disintegrating memory, deceptive prognostications and inaccurate hearsay, misleading accounts may also be based upon misinformation, misinterpretation and malicious manipulation.

One of the more memorable, presumably accurate, disclosures revealed that during frenzied coitus a couple inadvertently and unknowingly activated the emergency call system beside their bed. Alerted, security staff arrived to find the heaving lovers still enraptured and entwined.

In another undercover (pun intended) coupling a male resident suffered a heart attack while making love to a woman in that woman's apartment. Emergency personnel were summoned--but only after the lovers had hastily re-clothed themselves. Rushed to a hospital, the man did not survive. In his own apartment the man's unwary widow, oblivious to her husband's habitual philandering was awakened from slumber and enlightened by the paramedics.

For the most part elderly sex at Devonshire tends to be discrete. Practices and frequency may vary, but sexual activity is far from obsolete. Rarely discussed, both physical and emotional affection continue to be coveted and enjoyed. During a hushed, somewhat hesitant dinner table conversation I was made aware that, despite aging and increased physical limitations it is far from unique for elders to continue to seek sensual gratification; I learned that a significant number of my very proper eighty- and ninety-year old friends possess and utilize sex toys--mechanisms that I have (apparently naively) viewed with embarrassment whenever I receive unsolicited illustrated catalogues and emails offering them for sale.

While there are seniors who desire fully committed male-female relationships, there are others like myself who, having survived at least one heart wrenching loss, are reluctant to risk additional emotional trauma, who do not relish the commitment to and responsibility for an inevitably declining partner. While longing for the past, many of us welcome the independence, the serenity, the absence of complications that we find in emotional seclusion. Many of us are content, comfortable, even grateful, for the opportunity to be selfish, self-reliant, selfi-indulgent and self-centered.

36

Although I am aging, my Gemini disposition continues to define me. Typically, while trying to decide between a variety of options for repapering my bathroom walls, my ambivalence took over. To help me choose a replacement, I pinned a selection of samples to the walls. Depending upon the time of day and my mood at the moment, I favored one example, then another, then still another. Each design reflected a different aspect of my personality, another of my diverse stages in life. Each one was *me*, but a different me. Which me did I want to emphasize? Which choice would best complement my aging comfort zone?

A delicate floral design reflected my introverted but happy childhood. Two strikingly sophisticated textures evoked my lively married years. A bolder floral echoed my current home's bucolic surroundings. There were numerous additional choices. Following weeks of moody reflection and days of constantly varying convictions, I finally opted for the pretty but timid floral. Not because I found it the most pleasing, nor because it complemented the décor of my adjoining bedroom, but because it was persuasively less costly to install. A poor choice, I soon replaced it with one of the more dramatic designs, a pattern I continue to enjoy.

Self-indulgent and lazy, I possess a number of unlikely habits, typified by my continuing patronization of a rather seedy, only moderately hygienic beauty parlor. For years I have frequented the dingy salon, alternating between two affable but mediocre stylists who habitually wipe their noses with their bare hands, then disconcert me by manipulating my freshly shampooed tresses with potentially contaminated fingers.

In addition to questionable hygiene, the resulting hairdos are merely adequate. Nevertheless, the establishment does offer some advantages. The shop's location is convenient, and, as I become increasingly less mobile, its curbside storefront enables easy access. The price is reasonable, and, most significantly, the woman who shampoos my scalp gives a marvelous massage.

I consider the shop's appellation, "Beauty Parlor," a misnomer. The establishment is the antithesis of the sophisticated, polished coiffeurs of my early life. Despite the current fascination with shabby-chic, the shop, and its employees, while suitably shabby, are not at all chic. Operators, both male and female, sport untidy, unattractive and unbecoming hairstyles dyed in unusual, unflattering, and decidedly unnatural colors. Either shockingly obese or painfully anorexic, most are garbed in unflattering clothing that emphasizes every negative attribute. Overly revealing garments and elaborate, occasionally controversial tattoos are ubiquitous. Virtually the entire staff appears to be in desperate need of patronizing some other, better beauty salon.

A cautious hypochondriac, I am reluctant to dine in self-service venues. I have visions of fellow diners reaching into food platters with unclean hands or licking, then replacing, supposedly sanitary, reusable serving utensils and morsels of surreptitiously tasted food. All too frequently, I have encountered purportedly hot food, and presumably chilled food served inadequately and irresponsibly at room temperature. Suspect safety aside, buffets (especially the more elaborate ones), although visually and aromatically inviting, have never appealed to me. I tend to select an unwise and incompatible variety of sensually, but not always digestively, appealing dishes.

Of late, the coronavirus pandemic has revised my behavior and my lifestyle. Restricted to my apartment, I have no need for makeup or flattering clothing. Cosmetics, haircuts, constricting brassieres, and ornamental accessories have become superfluous.

Having adjusted to a revised and simplified way of life, I find myself ambivalent about an eventual return to previous habits, to a comparatively demanding lifestyle. My current regimen is less complicated and more relaxed. I am comfortable. I can be lazy. I do not have to fret about my appearance or the hospitality of my home. Although I miss friendly face-to-face interactions, I enjoy telephone visits. I am not bored. The internet keeps me abreast of the times. Lifelong hobbies occupy my leisure. I do not find myself at loose ends. I am content to be relatively idle. When the pandemic subsides and relative safety returns, I may not rush to reinstate all of my former routines.

Secluded, with no need to update my wardrobe and no longer patronizing multiple restaurants, my expenditures have dwindled dramatically. Providentially, unspent assets enable me to donate food and shelter to the less fortunate.

37

O bserving neighbors' visiting children, grandchildren, and great-grand-
children, I have concluded that there are two types of descendants
- selfless and selfish: those who care about and care for their elders, and those
who care exclusively about themselves, about the riddance of responsibility,
or the prospect of inheritance with the potential of personal gain.

It is a pleasure to watch supportive, sustaining family members encourage and enjoy their elders' late-life choices and commitments. Nevertheless,
even well-meaning descendants can disrupt and inadvertently diminish their
forbearer's ease and peace of mind. Following her husband's death, at the
behest of caring children, one of my neighbors relocated across the country
to reside near her middle-aged offspring. Having left established friendships
and a favorable climate for an unfamiliar environment, the lady became
lonely and discouraged. Regretting the move, she persuaded her children to
let her return to her previous locale. Once there, resettled and rejuvenated,
she revived a friendship with a recently widowed neighbor. Now married,
the couple enjoys a most affectionate and adventurous life together.

While children usually embrace or at least tolerate a widowed parent's Significant Other, greedy, manipulative descendants may contrive to destroy an elder's late-life, compensatory, consoling relationships.

The father of two ruthless sisters was living contentedly with his long-time mistress in an apartment near mine. One morning, after the elderly gentleman's physical health had begun to deteriorate ever so slightly, his callous daughters, having arrived unannounced from their homes in the northeast, abducted their traumatized father. The pair literally dragged the struggling man out of his apartment and along the hallway, essentially kidnapping him for transfer to a similar, if less costly, New England facility. Moaning and calling out in desperation, the beleaguered man begged a sturdy male neighbor for succor. Sadly, the neighbor was powerless to help. Shortly thereafter, without adequate means of support, the uprooted gentleman's abandoned, less-solvent mistress was obliged to vacate their comfortable apartment and the costly community. Concurrently the daughters intercepted and terminated all further contact between their ill-fated father and his erstwhile mate. Before long, separated, living in inferior quarters, and pining for one another, both victims passed away. Presumably, the daughters inherited their father's fortune.

In yet another incident, a kind and caring but ill-informed husband reluctantly prolonged the comatose life of his hospitalized wife for a number of futile years. Enlightened only months after she finally passed away, the widower confided that, unfortunately, while struggling to prevent his terminally ill spouse from suffering, he had been unaware of alternative compassionate options that, if authorized, could have terminated a hopeless, hapless existence by withdrawing life-prolonging tubes and treatments.

Conversely, at the end of her life, when my mother lay comatose in a hospital bed dependent upon life-sustaining equipment, I directed the employment of death delaying instruments and medications be maintained.

During preceding years, Mother had numerous opportunities to request terminal procedures, yet, because she conspicuously evaded those discussions, I presumed she would have opted to be kept alive as long as possible. Respectfully, if reluctantly, I instructed her physicians accordingly.

Whether one's potential survivors are ill-suited, ill-advised, or ill-motivated--even if they are fully capable and caring--I cannot stress strongly enough how important it is to create adequate legal and medical end-of-life provisions, whatever they may be; to instruct surrogates while one is still duly, certifiably--*and legally*--competent.

38

One of the more stimulating activities in my retirement community has been participating in a memoir-writing group. Monthly meetings comprising fewer than a dozen individuals were faithfully attended. (I use the term *individuals* wisely as each participant had his or her unique history and viewpoint.) Scenarios varied from a rural, outhouse-necessitated childhood to a Park Avenue penthouse; from two Holocaust survivors to a heroic participant in the World War II European underground; from an Olympic medalist to a self-made media mogul. Sharing intimate memories attendees bonded, developing an appreciative intimacy with one another.

For most participants, the motivation to recount their past was the preservation and dissemination of information for descendants and, in the process, the sharpening of potentially fading recall. Each month we were to write something new, then assemble to listen to each author read a brief excerpt from his or her recent jottings.

Recollections were surprisingly well written and nearly all were of genuine interest. Many were unexpectedly honest and revealing. Although criticism was forbidden one could always gain insight from others reactions. Demand for more information and questions about details afforded evidence that something had not been made sufficiently clear; laughter at an appropriate moment signaled approval; inappropriate laughter or the lack of laughter when humor was intended was cautionary; misinterpretation of a particular entry invited revision.

Eventually gatherings came to an end. As time passed, two of the participants died. One succumbed to dementia. Others, having recorded and shared all that they could or wished to recall, ceased to attend. Although an attempt was made to keep the group intact, when the inspiring but physically wearying chairperson retired the meetings drifted into oblivion.

While they lasted, the gatherings had an unanticipated beneficial effect on many of us. Joyful memories were happily relived while, writing about former troubles, we gained perspective and came to appreciate what challenges and hardships we had overcome. Belatedly a number of us realized long overdue pride in our capacity for survival. The passage of time became more friend than foe. We developed a sense of peace with our pasts and with ourselves. Enhanced bonding with children and grandchildren became a welcome bonus.

In attempting to recall our individual histories we recognized that all five of our senses --- sight, sound, taste, touch and smell--- could generate latent memories; could prompt us to revisit long overlooked places, emotions and events. The chance glimpse of an old photograph, the echo of a sentimental melody, the reminiscent flavor of a half-forgotten childhood treat, the caress of a sudden breeze, the whiff of a once familiar aroma might all engender latent recollections.

As a child I associated the odor of Cashmere Bouquet powder with my grandmother. Realizing that fragrance could be associated with and identify people and places, I resolved to acquire a signature scent of my own. By default, in childhood it was Johnson's Baby Powder. As a young adult, prompted by trips to Europe, I chose Lanvin's *Arpege*. During my

South American years, chiefly because my boyfriend Luiz Antonio liked it, my preferred perfume became Caron's *Fleur de Rocaille*. Following marriage to Joseph Jones, I identified with Estée Lauder's *Pleasures*.

Aromas may produce unanticipated, even controversial and incongruous reactions. Pleasant odors do not necessarily give rise to positive memories. Conversely, disagreeable aromas may awaken pleasurable reflections. I like the stench of raw sewage because it evokes happy times spent among the canals of Venice. Conversely, the pleasing aroma of pine needles depresses me, making me feel wistful, even lonely, as I relive childhood feelings of isolation caused by family-forbidden Christmas trees and prohibited yuletide celebrations. The pervasive odor of molten tar elates me because it reminds me of New York City in the 1940s when the springtime resurfacing of streets was concurrent with school letting out for the summer and the onset of freedom, vacations and adventure. The intoxicating fragrance of lilies takes me back to Paris where heady floral displays routinely welcomed me to the lobby of my customary hotel.

Music may arguably be the most powerful instigator of nostalgia. Whether classical or popular, orchestral or vocal, timeworn or recent, music invariably triggers a variety of moods, a multitude of memories. Despite widespread reliance on hearing aids and a propensity for declining recall, in my aging community the sound of visiting entertainers performing decades of familiar melodies inspires sing-alongs and gives rise to countless recollections. Even my most forgetful neighbors, some with Alzheimer's disease, can be glimpsed joining in, accurately mouthing every lyric.

The caress of a gentle breeze can be reminiscent of a bygone lover's tender touch.

Printed media may also jog one's memory. Recently a neighbor drew me aside to whisper that she had borrowed a copy of my memoir *Chance Encounters* from the library and, reading it, was reminded of a long suppressed episode in her youth. Her recollection had been triggered by a description of my teenage friendship with and affection for Arturo Toscanini's grandson Walfredo. My raconteur confided that, as an innocent college student, she had attended a weekend fraternity party at Yale University where she had been trapped and molested by an inebriated blind date. Struggling but seemingly defenseless against the apparent inevitability of rape, the frightened virgin, sobbing for help, had been rescued in the nick of time, calmed and escorted to safety by a "handsome, compassionate, and protective" underclassman named Toscanini. Her reference to Wally rekindled my recollection of one of his more astute observations: in Wally's opinion the most alluring attire a woman could wear was either a plunging (but not too plunging) neckline of dark velvet framing pale skin or clouds of pastel, illusively transparent chiffon. "A lady should never reveal too much, just hint," he advised, "Let a man see *almost* but not quite enough so that he yearns to undress her in order to see more."

39

I ronically, the less I have to do, and the older I become the faster time flies. Living in Florida with its mild, relatively consistent climate and decreasingly exigent lifestyle has corrupted my perception of time and the seasons. With ever-increasing speed, my days catapult into weeks, my months into years, and my years into decades. Despite my reduced activity and repetitive routines, rather than dragging, time seems to accelerate.

To identify the current day, I rely upon the labeled pillbox that apportions my daily assortment of medications. The compartmentalized container has become my *aide-memoire*. As each week concludes, the need to refill the box astounds me with the rapidity at which the previous seven days have vanished.

As a Floridian, my awareness of the changing seasons has become somewhat elusive, yet, due to chipped fingernails, I am always conscious of the arrivals of spring and fall. Resetting my considerable collection of timepieces to accommodate Daylight Savings Time inevitably wreaks havoc with my manicure. Somewhat less precise, the arrivals and departures of summer and winter are heralded by the arrivals and departures of vehicle-laden trucks relocating seasonal residents' automobiles.

Illustrative of the transformation between my northern and southern lifestyles is the contrast between my northern and southern dental offices. In Manhattan, my doctor practiced on a high floor in a midtown tower with views of other tall, gray, impersonal office buildings. In Florida, my dentist occupies a charming, New England-style cottage set in the midst of a lovely garden. During treatments, I gaze out at a birdbath surrounded by blossoming magnolia, bougainvillea, and multi-hued orchids. Dreariness and monotony have been supplanted by beauty. Boring has become pleasing.

Color continues to distinguish the seasons. Springtime is yellow, enhanced by blossoming cassia trees. Summer is dominated by vibrant red as the flamboyants flourish. Autumn and winter become lavender with wisteria and crepe myrtle, purple with plumbago. Multihued bougainvillea enhances the entire year.

Like the surrounding foliage, the color of socially acceptable clothing can vary with the seasons. Mimicking traditional, more northerly concepts of propriety, transplanted southerners frequently restrict white garments and accessories to summer months, emphasizing darker and more vivid, if sometimes less appropriate, apparel throughout the balance of the year. I wonder whether such clothing selections are merely fashionable or if they betray nostalgia for previous lives and lifestyles.

When I was a child, women and children customarily wore hats and gloves. Not merely the climate, but one's stage of life dictated sartorial selections. As they aged, my grandmother and her friends were confined to black, white, grey, and an occasional mourning lavender. Even after becoming a widow, my mother continued to wear colors of her choice and guardedly more contemporary designs. My only considerations have been whether a particular shade or style becomes me and is appropriate for my current mood or imminent activity.

Men's wardrobes have also undergone modification and modernization. Everyday outfits have become more comfortable, more casual, and less restrictive. Obsolete are my father's stiffly starched shirt collars, gratuitous vests, and pocket watch with dangling fob. Men's overly modest, chest-concealing bathing suits have been supplanted by Speedos. Clean-shaven faces and elegantly groomed facial hair have been supplemented by scruffy stubble that, in my opinion, merely makes men look slovenly and in need of a bath.

While I have no desire to return to the past, I am old and crotchety enough to view today's styles as excessively casual and self-accentuating. Modesty and maturation no longer seem to go hand in hand. Evolving as succeeding generations inevitably do, today's young adults, with their blatant tattoos, deliberately distressed clothing, and frequently unflattering, overly revealing, potentially distracting garments, seem desperate for attention, portraying themselves as self-centered, self-promoting narcissists. They seem to emphasize the *me* rather than *mankind*, the *self* rather than *society*, to be *takers* rather than *partakers*.

I miss the more relaxed tempo, the decency, dignity and decorum, the restraint and presumed honesty of the twentieth century. Perhaps times were not better then, but with information slower and harder to come by, we were less aware and marginally less troubled. I find a number of the evolving twenty-first-century styles and strategies--alleged advances--disappointing and somewhat disconcerting.

40

Gazing out the window one afternoon, I noticed a truck approach the service entrance of my residence, presumably to deliver furniture to one of my neighbors. Displayed across the rear doors, I saw the decorating firm's logo, a reassuring reminder that "Upholsterers never die, they always recover."

With advancing age and diminishing vigor, it becomes necessary to conserve energy, to differentiate desire from fantasy, the realistic from the unrealistic, the feasible from the improbable, to expend one's vitality upon the likely rather than the unlikely. While going out still feels good, coming home may feel even better.

The frequently frustrating anxiety to satisfactorily modify one's daily routine is a common characteristic of advancing age. In search of significant rewarding activity to assuage decreasing ability and increasing leisure, one may fret over selecting appropriate alternative occupations.

A number of my priorities and interests have changed. I have begun to watch television and peruse daily newspapers more selectively. With a shorter attention span, accompanied by increasingly limited patience and faster fatiguing eyes, my choices are dictated by the useful rather than the abstract, by the pertinent rather than the irrelevant. No longer cooking, I ignore recipes but pay more attention to restaurant reviews. No longer eager to tour, to spend significant time abroad, previously tempting travel articles and enticing catalogs have ceased to merit my attention. The perusing of obituaries that might require acknowledgment has become mandatory. To maintain mental health, accompanied by a fistful of sharp pencils (with erasers), the challenge of solving puzzles has become of prime importance.

As responsibilities and obligations diminish, I find aging to be a time of relative leisure, an opportunity for increased self-indulgence. As attitudes toward dining and diet modify, some people become more cautious, hoping to extend the length and quality of their lives. Others, feeling they have little to lose, take pleasure indulging in delicious, if insalubrious, repasts.

As habits change, as values and cautions adjust, I am comfortable with my revised lifestyle. It feels appropriate to retreat into a less assertive, less energetic routine. Always cautious and low-key, I am becoming even more so. I find a certain comfort in advancing age. Previous pressures--the discomfort of tight girdles, the hazard of high-heeled shoes, the angst of recurring stress--have become avoidable. I am beginning to accept rather than compete, to relax, to evade much that is undesirable. Tranquility is replacing anxiety; old age is becoming an indulgence.

41

S ince I began writing this memoir the world has changed. A planet-wide pandemic --- the coronavirus virus --- has compromised the globe.

Current constraints remind me of the 1940s and early 1950s when, primarily as a consequence of the Second World War, lives and lifestyles were gradually but significantly transformed. As in the mid twentieth century, of necessity if reluctantly, routines and traditions of everyday life are being altered.

In the 1940s, wartime life, rife with fear and sacrifice, was often unpleasant. Significant difficulties and deprivations had to be endured. Those of us who are old enough to remember, tend to forget how troubled, pessimistic, even fearful, we once were. Nevertheless, we survived. While the recovery, the readjustment, was slow, often irregular, we stumbled forward. Our temporarily constrained world evolved into the one that we are currently fearful of loosing. Once again, we appear to be on the brink of new disciplines, new practices and new concepts. Hopefully, forthcoming changes will be for the better.

World War II, with its education expanding GI Bill of Rights and inclusion of women like Rosie the Riveter into the workforce, spawned an expansion of the middle class. Families were reunited; tranquil domesticity was emphasized. The first pre-planned, mass-produced suburban residential community, Long Island's Levittown, became a prototype for flourishing postwar suburbia.

Although the self-perceptions and ambitions of young women began to expand, media initially ignored the fact that females wished to assume employment and importance beyond their homes. Despite changing attitudes, for almost a decade radio and television situation comedies like *Father Knows Best, Make Room for Daddy* and *The Adventures of Ozzie and Harriet* continued to portray families with caring, dominant fathers; doting, docile mothers, and obedient children. Advertisements continued to feature apron-clad wives promoting everyday products in household settings. Verbal and visual media censorship was rigorous. Vulgar vocabulary and suggestive innuendo were forbidden. Televised married couples had to occupy twin beds, always prudently separated by a night table. The permissiveness of today's social media would have horrified mid-twentieth century viewers.

Paradoxically, those family oriented postwar years spawned increasingly blatant sexuality. Bikini bathing suits were introduced and a profusion of alluring Miss Subway posters featuring Jinx Falkenberg, the initial Miss Rheingold, enhanced countless subway cars.

Gradually, women were acquiring enhanced status and respect. On radio talk shows, wives began to costar with their husbands. In 1940, supermodel Falkenberg together with her husband, newsman Tex McCrary, initiated a popular couple-hosted talk show. A few years later the format included *Breakfast with Dorothy and Dick*, staring producer Dick Kollmar and his wife, the popular columnist and television quiz show panelist Dorothy Kilgallen.

Will current concerns and restrictions engender comparable changes? Will caution replace cozy; casual replace formal? Will expansive celebrations subside into more cautious festivity? Will home offices continue to replace crowded workspaces? Will smiling, nods and elbow-taps replace handshakes? Will sanitizers and constant hand washing continue and escalate the need for restorative lotions? Will protective facemasks that conceal emotions, continue to muffle conversations and hinder lip-reading?

42

Recently I happened across a book by radio and TV personality Steve Harvey entitled *Act Like a Lady, Think Like a Man*. I felt that its title described my mother to perfection! Born in 1893 and raised with three assertive and competitive older brothers, in her desire and determination to achieve gender neutrality and equality with her male siblings she was ahead of her time.

Based upon her disposition and her behavior I grew up believing that men comprised the physically stronger, protective sex while women constituted the wiser, more insightful, more efficacious sex. My perception of the world and the people in it was based upon maternal example. In addition to my modestly educated mother with her sharp mind, sound instincts and fundamental commonsense I was raised by a grandmother who, despite minimal formal schooling, was practical and profound. Both women had innate wisdom. Because my robust, intelligent, and extremely well-educated father traveled a great deal he had a protective and affectionate, if less significant, influence on my day-to-day life. I considered being born female a distinct advantage rather than a disadvantage; I was grateful to have been born a woman, a sensible woman, rather than a more responsibility encumbered man. I was amused by a sign in the hallway leading to the restrooms of a neighborhood bistro that instructed, "Men go to the left, women to the right (because they're always right)."

During my youth the term "glass ceiling" referred to the upper portion of a plant filled hothouse. Through the years the term has acquired both political and social significance. It has come to represent a controversial concept in regard to the merits of males versus females. Compared to other nations the presumably advanced United States has been surprisingly laggard in appreciating the power and potential of women. Elsewhere, in addition to historically significant queens and empresses such as Cleopatra of Egypt, Christina of Sweden, Catherine of Russia, Cici of China, Victoria and Elizabeth of England, nations have chosen impressive women such as Indira Gandhi of India, Golda Meyer of Israel, Margaret Thatcher of the United Kingdom, Benazir Bhutto of Pakistan and Andrea Merkel of Germany as their leaders.

My earliest memory of an American woman daring to campaign for the presidency of the United States --- albeit not seriously --- dates back to 1940. At a time when incumbent Franklin Roosevelt was officially being challenged by Wendell Willkie, comedienne Gracie Allen, ran as a candidate of the Sunrise Party whose logo was a kangaroo with the motto, "It's in the bag." Cheerfully Gracie would proclaim, "Everybody knows a woman is better than a man when it comes to introducing bills into the house," then observe that "every politician must be able to keep both feet on the fence."

In the United States women have enjoyed a haphazard professional and political history. Prior to women's suffrage, in 1872 Victoria Woodhill, competing against Frederick Douglass, attempted unsuccessfully to become the first female presidential candidate. In 1884, on a different minor ticket, Marietta Stow became the initial female vice-presidential candidate. In 1940 Margaret Chase Smith became the first woman to serve in both houses of Congress and in 1964 she competed unsuccessfully for the Republican presidential nomination. In 1972, Shirley Chisholm of New York, the first African American elected to Congress, vied unsuccessfully for the Democratic presidential nomination and Elizabeth Dole flirted briefly with the possibility of a Republican candidacy in 1999. In 2016, while far from the first woman to seek election to the White House, former First Lady/Secretary of State Hillary Clinton became the initial viable female candidate.

I would never vote for a candidate on the basis of his or her sexual identity. I endorse the person whom I believe will do the best job. People are people --- good, bad, indifferent, capable or incapable. They should succeed or fail according to their abilities and their philosophies, not their gender or the color of their skin.

Throughout the contentious Trump-Clinton campaign, both Clinton and her ultimately successful opponent inspired enthusiastic admirers and equally ardent detractors.

Media coverage of the 2016 campaign coincided with articles pertaining to the *#MeToo* movement, to accusations of sexual harassment in the workplace. Increasingly, particularly in the entertainment industry, women were confiding and confronting incidents of repugnant male manipulation; feminist views and feminist rights were becoming an increasing source of disclosure, discourse and contention.

When I graduated from college, along with my contemporaries I knew that far too frequently the accessibility and advancement of a chosen career (particularly one in glamorous fields such as acting and modeling) might be facilitated and enhanced by sexual compromise. We were all cognizant of the Casting Couch. Involuntary intercourse, however reluctant and repulsive, was an anticipated choice; comply or risk rejection. Too often career advancement became about how one chose to value oneself and one's ambitions. While men in persuasive positions have not changed appreciably, women's leverage and compliance have been evolving. Silence and the acceptance of maltreatment are diminishing. Although I view the increasing exposure, condemnation and castigation of predators as long overdo, I do not appreciate the hypocritical criticism voiced by those women who knowingly and willingly continue to cooperate with men purely to advance and satisfy personal ambitions or to falsely seek recompense and publicity. While far too many innocent victims are being molested and are in genuine need of sympathy and succor, I believe that covetous cooperators and attention seekers are not uniformly entitled to recourse, recompense or sympathy.

43

To one degree or another, during most of my adult life I have been involved in politics. In 1945, when I was a relatively immature thirteen years of age, President Franklin Delano Roosevelt's death triggered my political consciousness. I felt as though I was losing a family member, a protective grandfather, that my world was about to change.

Despite my close relationship with Manhattan Borough President Edgar J. Nathan, Jr., and scattered encounters with Harry Truman, Dwight Eisenhower, and Thomas Dewey, it was only in the early 1950s, through my business-initiated friendship with Nelson Rockefeller, that I became actively involved in the world of politics and politicians.

Nelson sponsored my introduction to and association with an increasing variety of candidates and office holders, to activities that included campaigning, poll watching, voter verification, and fund raising. In 1971, (as an independent voter but a registered Republican), I was elected to a relatively inconsequential New York State administrative position. While my moderately liberal opinions endure, due to ever more challenging national and international concerns my enthusiasms and my loyalties have changed.

Having become a registered Democrat, I regard the twenty-first century with increasing wariness.

I view Donald Trump's ascendancy, combined with the machinations of Vladimir Putin, Kim Jong-un, and an assortment of other heads of state, as a galvanizing factor in the world's upheaval. I view Trump, in particular, as Fate's means for instituting and hastening inevitable change. I believe, through what I see as his ignorance, arrogance, greed, self-deception, fundamental dishonesty, and delusion--his seeming lunacy--that he will hasten the eventual destruction of the world as we know it. Like the evil, if charismatic, Adolf Hitler, who reconfigured the twentieth century, I believe Trump may possibly (perhaps inadvertently) instigate a global war. I foresee his policies regarding weaponry, war, healthcare, and climate change as accelerating loss of life, aggravating the spread of illness, depleting our fresh air, food, water supplies and, ultimately, if extremely remotely, engendering a potential devastation of our planet.

Trump's unconscionable *modus operandi* of divide-and-conquer, his improbable threats and promises, his apparent delusions, devious and distracting lawsuits, contentious lying, petty petulance, and massive misdirection will, I fear, prove--at least temporarily--catastrophic. In Donald Trump, I see a twisted mind, a warped individual. I believe the former President, consistently manipulative and corrupt, has significant previous criminal activity to conceal, that he is desperate to obscure a plethora of punishable crimes perpetrated not only by himself, but also by his father, his children, and their spouses. The compulsive "Prevaricator in Chief" brings to mind former Senator Daniel Patrick Moynihan's dictum: "Everyone is entitled to his own opinion, but not to his own facts."

During the coronavirus pandemic, our deliberately divisive President was motivated by self-interest, self-preservation, and the preservation of power rather than by the preservation of American lives. Trump's lifelong

philosophy of "divide and conquer," engendering fear in order to dominate, threatened to destroy our country. I felt as though I no longer lived
in a democracy, but in an autocracy, in a United States no longer a haven
"of the people, by the people and for the people." Reluctantly, I fear that
regaining our republic may require considerably more time and effort than
fellow Americans anticipate. Conventional attitudes and traditions may be
slow to reinstate.

When would-be-dictator Trump--aided and abetted by a self-serving
and cowardly congress--diminished the world's positive perception of the
United States, I became reluctant to travel abroad, ashamed to be identified
by a passport issued by the USA.

The United States of yesteryear--compassionate, idealistic, welcoming, and protective--the democracy, of which I have always been so proud,
has been transformed. Ruled by the egocentric and the greedy, the nation
is becoming increasingly devoid of moral rectitude. Few genuine statesmen
remain. Rather than inspiring the best in people, the worst is not merely
condoned but encouraged. Manipulating twenty-first-century media, the for-
ty-fifth president carefully cultivated and encouraged the worst in people. All
too often, "divide and conquer" replaced "unify and liberate." Increasingly,
the entire world around us, plagued by poverty, turmoil, and dysfunction,
appears to need restructuring. Reluctantly, I fear a global war may not only
be inevitable but necessary.

Always fortunate, I am not overly concerned about my personal
well-being in a universe that may be destined for imminent if temporary,
disaster. Throughout history, empires have risen, dominated, prevailed, and
eventually declined. I sense that the time has come for the United States
to relinquish primacy. Demotion is not necessarily a calamity and need
not be a disaster. Good can rise out of evil; positive can supplant negative.
Today's increasingly turbulent planet needs refreshing, renewal, and repair,

revitalization and restructuring. A fundamental optimist, I am neither overly discouraged nor distraught about the eventual outcome.

44

Most of my mistakes in life have been relatively innocent, the result of ignorance, idiocy, or inertia rather than malevolence. While I have become more skeptical, more apprehensive, and more suspicious, I have also become less scrutinizing and less vigilant. Paradoxically, both caution and susceptibility have become more pronounced. As I become more retiring and detached, my shortcomings multiply, and my acuity lessens.

I am attempting to make my dwindling days as tranquil, as free of challenges and negativity as possible. I am trying to maintain an unencumbered and unthreatened existence. While I strive to isolate and insolate myself from perceived negativity and discouraging intrusions, I am sometimes too impatient, too intolerant, and overly critical of others in my desire to avoid unpleasantness. One of my neighbors advises that when life seems to be deteriorating, one has a choice; one may "get bitter or get better." As years accumulate, a positive agenda, while potentially more difficult, becomes increasingly essential.

It is important to distinguish between the plausible and the implausible, the possible and the impossible. I must discipline and ration my emotional energy as I do my physical energy; I must differentiate between fantasy and delusion.

Increasingly, I find comfort and guidance in religion. Although I rarely participate in formal ceremony, I consider myself devout. Despite some misgivings about organized faith, I am a believer. Rarely taking part in communal worship, I pray regularly, but privately, in gratitude; occasionally in supplication.

I believe that most faiths were conceived to protect and inspire rather than divide and destroy. The Golden Rule--"do onto others as you would have others do onto you" --is basic to virtually all denominations. Paraphrased, the directive is not merely fundamental to Christianity, but to Judaism, Islam, Buddhism, Hinduism, Confucianism, and Taoism, among others. Devised to make the world a kinder, more tolerant, and tolerable place, spiritual strategies should inspire and encourage forbearance, security, and a more tranquil humanity. Religion should protect and inspire rather than dispute and divide; it should neither camouflage nor excuse hatred and abuse.

While I respect the pageantry and camaraderie of religious ritual, for me my faith is not so much about doctrine and display as it is about comfort, inner peace, and security, about support and reassurance.

45

Although the trials and tribulations of aging often seem personal and unique, repressed feelings of sadness and frustration are not uncommon. Negative concerns and sentiments are not rare.

Whether subtle or pronounced, hidden or overt, negative emotions need to be confronted. Temperamentally as well as physically, one must adjust to changes. One may need to distract oneself, to search for purpose, to expose oneself to new experiences, to revise and expand one's options. Burdensome responsibilities that follow the loss of a spouse may require excessive, often unfamiliar, attention but that effort may also be a blessing, it may occupy and engross.

It is up to each of us to insure ourselves against potential problems and deterioration. It is up to us to confront our negatives and attempt to overcome or neutralize them. When reflecting upon the past, we must not pine for what we have lost, but recall and take pride in what we have achieved. As a label on the rear window of a car parked next to mine instructs, "wag more, bark less."

To quote Shakespeare, "our past is prologue." Our present is paramount; our future imminent. There may be an urgency to utilize the remainder of our lives productively, to avoid ennui while adding significance to our remaining days. Some of us may attempt to reinvent ourselves, to acquire new techniques, to conquer fresh challenges. Others wish to enhance, recapture, or revise proven talents. As one ages, there may be an incompatibility between one's desires and ability, between the aspiration to achieve more and the capacity to accomplish less. There may be a yearning to repay past blessings, to validate one's time on earth. Courting justification for our existence, we may speculate about eventual obituaries, wishing to enhance and enrich memories that family and surviving acquaintances will sustain.

As one ages, reliance upon family members is not always feasible. One should supplement the intimacy of relatives with additional confidants. Friendships become more significant not merely as diversion and entertainment, but as insurance against isolation and lack of compassionate oversight should one ever require aid or protection from oneself or from others.

Some of us attempt to reinvent ourselves, to acquire new techniques, to conquer fresh challenges. Others may wish to augment, recapture, or revise proven talents. As one ages, there may be an incompatibility between one's desires and ability, between the aspiration to achieve more and the capacity to accomplish less. There may be a yearning to repay past blessings, to validate one's time on earth. Courting justification for our existence, we may speculate about eventual obituaries, wishing to enhance and enrich memories that family and surviving acquaintances will sustain.

With advancing age and diminishing vigor, it becomes necessary to conserve energy, to differentiate desire from fantasy, the realistic from the unrealistic, the feasible from the improbable, to expend one's vitality upon the likely rather than the unlikely.

The frequently frustrating anxiety to satisfactorily modify one's daily routine is a common characteristic of advancing age. In search of significant rewarding activity to assuage decreasing ability and increasing leisure, one may fret over selecting appropriate alternative occupations.

As responsibilities and obligations diminish, I find aging to be a time of relative leisure, an opportunity for increased self-indulgence. As attitudes toward dining and diet modify, some people become more cautious, hoping to extend the length and quality of their lives. Others, feeling they have little to lose, take pleasure indulging in delicious, if insalubrious, repasts.

As habits change, as values and cautions adjust, I am comfortable with my revised lifestyle. It feels appropriate to retreat into a less assertive, less energetic routine. Always cautious and low-key, I am becoming even more so. I find a certain comfort in advancing age. Previous pressures--the discomfort of tight girdles, the hazard of high-heeled shoes, the angst of recurring stress--have become avoidable. I am beginning to accept rather than compete, to relax, to evade much that is undesirable. Tranquility is replacing anxiety; old age is becoming an indulgence.

46

Despite modifications in my physical and intellectual energy, in my memory, and my thinking patterns, I feel that I am still fundamentally unchanged, an involved and caring human being looking forward to a future of worlds yet to be conquered and a *raison d'etre* to justify.

Daily newspapers provide a constant reminder of time's passage. Birthday tributes congratulate fewer and fewer celebrants who have reached or exceeded my age; obituaries portray a preponderance of people who, although elderly, were significantly younger than I am when they passed away.

With reasonably good health, I find that growing old need not be nearly as limiting or unappealing as one may have been led to expect. While some doors close, others open to compensate. I recall the nonagenarian comedian George Burns--whom I met and chatted with aboard a charter flight from Los Angeles to New York--observing that, "You can't help getting older, but you don't have to get old," while a reassuring sign on the wall of my podiatrist's waiting room asserts that "You don't stop laughing because you grow old, you grow old because you stop laughing."

Recently, an unexpected reminder of time's passage arrived on my doorstep. The trademark-blue Tiffany box, embellished with white satin ribbons, contained a pair of lovely crystal champagne flutes, a gift from American Express to acknowledge and appreciate sixty years of my continuous use of their credit card. Countless trips to Bloomingdales and overseas flea markets; innumerable passages aboard airplanes and ocean liners --- but six decades? How astonishing! My convenience and loyalty were being rewarded but, while simultaneously surprised by and grateful for the gift, I suddenly felt many years older than I had before it arrived.

Always introspective, I presumed that, in writing a memoir, I would merely be recording a familiar image of myself, that the undertaking would entail recollection rather than recognition. Instead, the project turned out to be an adventure of discovery, of revelation. I found myself more interesting and more worthwhile than anticipated, more complex, more involved, and more evolved.

Still, my self-image and self-evaluation continue to fluctuate. Paradoxically, I perceive myself as both invincible and invisible, as worthy and useless, as valued yet of minimal significance. When reliving disappointments, I am still coming to terms with myself.

I empathize with a neighbor who, pointing to the laugh lines around her eyes and the furrows across her brow, commented that "These aren't wrinkles, they're a map of where I've been."

I have been to many places and encountered a multitude of diverse situations. Blessed with loving, indulgent parents, a stress-free childhood, financial security even in questionable times, a diverse assortment of friends and acquaintances, a lifetime of extraordinary experiences that included worldwide travel and edifying exposure to diverse cultures, I have much to reflect upon, and a great deal for which to be grateful.

Like others of increasing years and decreasing capability, I am modifying my lifestyle. I have become more cautious. Although blessed with reasonably good health, out of necessity, I have become more anticipatory, wary, circumspect, self-protective and resourceful.

My generation has survived a complex, often intriguing era. The *mise en scène* of our lives--worldwide conflict offset by significant technical and artistic achievement and debatable moral modification--has molded us. During our lifetime, the world has changed dramatically. Despite many positive changes, with the proliferation of environmental contamination, mounting global strife and dissatisfaction, increasing impatience and increasingly destructive methods of combat, with the spawning of inappropriate and ill-advised world leaders, I fear for the future. Reluctantly, having lived through the best of times, I anticipate (at least temporarily) a potential worst of times. Nostalgic for what I perceive as the relative ease of the past, I envision the likelihood of a deteriorating future, yet remain considerably too curious to wish to hasten my own demise.

Too often, one may wait until evening to appreciate how fine the day has been. By chance, the windows of my homes have always been oriented eastward, embracing and welcoming the sunrise, the promise and wonder of a new day. In my current (and presumably my final) dwelling, the windows face north and west, displaying spectacular sunsets, explosions of color that fade slowly and gently into the darkness of night. I find comfort and contentment in the captivating twilight, in the gradual, dwindling beauty of the evening sky. Why should the fading of my own existence be any less routine, less normal, less inevitable, less acceptable than the fading of the day?